SERVING THE CHURCH

The Lay Eucharistic Minister's Handbook

Other titles in the *Serving the Church* series:

A Handbook for Children's Liturgy Barbara Mary Hopper

Forthcoming:

The School Governor's Handbook

A Handbook for Catechists

Reading in Church: A Handbook

Practical Parish Administration

SERVING THE CHURCH

Series Editors: Michael and Kathleen Walsh

The Lay Eucharistic Minister's Handbook

Ann Tomalak

CANTERBURY
PRESS
Norwich

© Ann Tomalak 2003

First published in 2003 by the Canterbury Press Norwich
(a publishing imprint of Hymns Ancient & Modern Limited,
a registered charity)
St Mary's Works, St Mary's Plain
Norwich, Norfolk, NR3 3BH

www.scm-canterburypress.co.uk

British Library Cataloguing in Publication Data

A catalogue record for this book is available
from the British Library

Bible quotations are taken from:
The New Jerusalem Bible
published and © 1985 by Darton, Longmann and Todd Ltd
and Doubleday and Co. Inc.

ISBN 1-85311-550-9

Typeset by Rowland Phototypesetting Ltd,
Bury St Edmunds, Suffolk
Printed and bound in Great Britain by
Biddles Ltd, www.biddles.co.uk

Contents

Serving the Church: A Series Introduction

This is one of a series of handbooks designed to help lay people play a greater part in the life of the Church. It is usual nowadays to find lay men and women reading at Mass, administering Communion, organizing children's liturgy, even sometimes leading eucharistic services in the absence of a priest. Lay people commonly organize the music for Mass and other liturgical events in the parish. Many are asked to help out in other ways, sometimes even outside the boundaries of the parish, by becoming, for example, governors of the local Catholic school.

For all these tasks, and other roles that the laity now play, the authors of the books in this series have tried to describe what is entailed in the particular role or ministry to which you have been called. They have provided something of the history and the theology where appropriate. They understand that people are willing, but often need encouragement to take on tasks that, in the past, may have seemed the special preserve of the clergy.

They also understand that those approached to undertake these ministries are often busy people with jobs to do and families to care for. The books are therefore as concise as it is possible to make them, written in straightforward language with a minimum of technical jargon (though glossaries are supplied where necessary) and include a good deal of practical advice.

We hope that these books will be helpful, not just in the practical details of fulfilling a ministry within the Church, but also in developing a deeper, more spiritual understanding of the mysteries of the Catholic faith.

Kathleen and Michael Walsh

Introduction

From the time of the apostles, Christians have gathered together for worship and mutual support. The New Testament model community meets each day for prayer and teaching and weekly for a ritual memorial meal. Its members serve one another, giving according to their abilities and resources, and receiving according to need. They preach the good news in words and by the way they live.

Even now, this would be our ideal for a parish community. We still use images of interdependence to describe ourselves. For example, we speak of being the many parts of one body (and Christ as the head of that body), stones built together and the fruitful branches of the one vine. Sharing one life in Christ, we would be foolish to cut ourselves off from others. Working together for the common good, everyone benefits. Supporting one another, all are lifted up.

The oldest-known liturgical texts show that Sunday was, from the beginning, *the* day for Christians to gather together for worship. Before any other feasts developed, Sunday was the great celebration of Christ's saving work, and this was repeated weekly. It was the day of resurrection, the day of creation, a foretaste of eternity. Christians felt obliged to be there from a deep sense of thanksgiving and praise, not by any law.

The twenty-first century is seeing something of a return to such attitudes. Fewer Catholics now think it a grave sin to miss Sunday Mass, so we may assume that the people in church have chosen to be there. It is a sign of hope that so many appreciate the fellowship at Sunday Mass – they come to worship God, to hear and respond to the readings, for Communion *and* to do these things in the company of others. This sense of togetherness is an integral part of a healthy Christian life. When we gather for Sunday worship, we are most fully the body of Christ, the Church.

At Mass we are fed first at the 'table of the word'. God's word is 'broken open' for us, so that we may share it, receive it, assimilate it, be nourished by it and so be strengthened to live as Christians. The scriptures challenge us. Though they reveal our weaknesses, they do it in the light of God's unceasing love for us. This encounter calls forth from us an authentic response in faith, sometimes sorrowful, sometimes joyful, and always a deepening of the relationship between Christ and his Church. He is the Word.

Only then can we be fed at the eucharistic table and receive the body and blood of Christ. We share his life. We are made one family, one community. With thanksgiving, we confess him as our Saviour and our Lord. The new covenant in his blood binds us to serve the one who called himself *our* servant. Christ, who is both priest and sacrifice, strengthens us to go out to do his work.

Christ is present in the word we share; in the consecrated bread and wine; in the priest who represents him at the altar; but, first and foremost, he is present in our gathering for worship. When the community assembles, Christ is there. Every liturgical celebration is the joint action of Christ and his Church.

These themes of community, service and worship are at the heart of this book. Through baptism we were incorporated into the body of Christ, the Church, we joined a worshipping community and we were made imitators of our Servant Lord. In our turn, we must serve too or, to use a synonym, minister.

You may be reading this book because you have been invited to become a lay eucharistic minister for your Roman Catholic parish community and want to know what is expected of you. Alternatively, perhaps you already serve your parish in this way and want to think about your ministry more deeply. Some of what follows may already be familiar to you; other parts will not be relevant to your particular community and you can safely skip over them.

This book was written by a lay eucharistic minister for other lay eucharistic ministers, present and future. Its aim is to explore with you not only what we do, but also the understandings that underpin our actions. Much of it is written using the word 'we' to remind you constantly that eucharistic ministers work together in, and for, the parish community.

Although you may be tempted to read straight through this book, you will find it more helpful to read a chapter at a time, then pause to think about the text and ponder the questions at the end. If you are reading the book as a group, let the questions act as discussion starters. Don't worry if you don't reach any firm conclusions. They are to help you assimilate the material and relate it to your specific situation. Above all, try to pray after each chapter, as an individual or in a group.

Before you go any further, take a moment now to think about, and pray for, your own parish community (or the community you will serve as a eucharistic minister). Then, as you continue with this book, keep in mind the real people whom you will serve, their hopes and needs.

What do Lay Eucharistic Ministers do?

Just about every Catholic in this country has seen a lay eucharistic minister at work. Most see them weekly, some daily. All but a very few are happy to receive Communion from a lay person. Younger people do not even remember a time when only the priest gave Communion. Thus, in general terms, we all know what lay eucharistic ministers do, even if we could not replicate their work without some training.

We understand that they are faithful Catholics with a distinctive liturgical role. They have been commissioned but not ordained. Otherwise, they are people like us, possibly friends and neighbours, but certainly not 'holier than thou'. We could do what they do.

Liturgy and ministry

Liturgy is the Church's public worship. The root meaning of the word is 'work of the people' and thus we are to be actively engaged in it. In the often quoted words of the Vatican II document on liturgy (*Sacrosanctum Concilium*), 'Mother Church earnestly desires that all the faithful should be led to that full, conscious and active participation in liturgical celebrations which is demanded by the very nature of the liturgy, and to which the Christian people, "a chosen race, a royal priesthood, a holy nation, a redeemed people" (1 Peter 2:9) have a right and obligation by reason of their baptism' (14).

Baptism makes us all servants, because it makes us one with Jesus Christ, who did not come to be served but to serve and give his life in the service of others. It is an honourable role; we are not drudges or slaves, but assistants and representatives of our Lord. Another word for servant is 'minister' (government ministers are national servants).

> Through baptism, the lay faithful are made one body with Christ ... They are, in their own way, made sharers in the priestly, prophetic and kingly office of Christ. They carry out their own part in the mission of the whole Christian people with respect to the Church and the world.
>
> *Christifideles Laici*, 9

All Christians are called to minister, though we have tended to reserve the word for certain kinds of work within the Church, specifically the ordained ministry. When we are being good neighbours, friends, parents and colleagues, we rarely see ourselves as Christlike or put a fancy name to what we are doing (though perhaps if we did the laity would be more valued). We do now talk about 'liturgical ministers', meaning all those who assist the community's worship – presider, servers, readers, cantors and musicians, eucharistic ministers and others, some ordained and some not.

In the early Church, ministry was viewed as a *charism*, a gift from God. There were many different gifts, many different ways of serving and all were needed. Every area of life, including liturgy, required the active collaboration of the whole community – those with different gifts working together for the common good.

Liturgical ministry is not an elite form of service, though it is special because it is such a privilege to serve God and one's community in this way. Liturgy is never a private act as every believer present should, by their own participation, also be helping others to get caught up in it. However, those who have specific tasks in the community's celebration also have a special duty to act faithfully and responsibly, because liturgy is the summit of all the Church's activity and the source of all her power (see *Sacrosanctum Concilium*, 10). Liturgical ministers shape and foster our worship. This prayer in common forms the faith that we express in the way we live each day.

An extraordinary ministry?

For many centuries, the Church seemed to forget that lay people had an active part to play in liturgy. So, when it was decided that the laity should again give Communion, they were called 'extraordinary' ministers of Communion. This was not meant to suggest a remarkable or surprising ministry, but it was simply that, at the time, the usual ('ordinary') giver of Communion was a deacon, priest or bishop. Now we prefer to use the plain term 'lay minister'.

When lay people began to give Communion in modern times, it was not always presented as their proper ministry, more as necessity. The Church had already reversed the traditional order of the sacraments of initiation, allowing children to come to Communion before they were confirmed. The customary tie with confession was relaxed so that adults who had received Communion infrequently were encouraged to do so every time they came to Mass. Then Communion under both kinds was restored to the people. It was easy enough to assume that the clergy needed help if the Communion rite was not to take too long, and this was often how lay ministers were introduced to parishes.

The role of the lay minister

It has taken time for us to understand that lay eucharistic ministers have their own specific role. They are not 'Father's little helpers', nor are they taking on a clerical function as the number of ordained clergy decreases.

At a parish Mass, they foster a sense of the one body of Christ by sharing Communion in a dignified and respectful way with many people in a relatively short space of time. They can also lead Communion services in the absence of a priest – not as a poor substitute for Mass but as a positive way for people to receive Communion frequently. This is particularly important to sick and housebound parishioners who may only receive occasional visits from a priest. In particular, those unable to get to church can participate most fully in the parish's Sunday Eucharist every week when a lay minister brings them Communion straight from Mass. Occasionally, a lay minister will have the privilege of giving Communion for the last time to someone who is dying – we call it *viaticum*, sustenance for the final journey to God.

> Greater access to Holy Communion should be made possible so that the faithful, by sharing more fully in the fruits of the sacrifice of the Mass, might dedicate themselves more readily and effectively to God and to the good of the Church and of humanity.
>
> *Immensae Caritatis*, 1973

Most lay eucharistic ministers are commissioned for and serve in their own parish, but some minister in religious houses, schools, hospitals or prisons – usually because they live or work there. Trained lay ministers may also be commissioned for a single eucharistic celebration away from their usual place of ministry (at a conference, perhaps, or on pilgrimage).

Lay eucharistic ministers are not paid for their service, which is freely offered. Job opportunities are beginning to open up within the Church and it is possible that in the future we will see more lay chaplains in schools and other institutions who will exercise a variety of liturgical and other ministries in the course of their work. For the present, though, lay eucharistic ministers will typically give Communion at Sunday Mass and, perhaps, spare an hour more to visit somebody who is sick.

They need to be prayerful people, living a Christian life, but not necessarily with time on their hands. It can be a terrific witness to see busy young adults and working parents making the commitment to organize their lives around ministry at Sunday Mass.

Eucharistic ministers offer honourable service to their communities. Their work is practical and witnesses to their faith. They have the privilege of recognizing Christ in others by sharing him with others, and so they help to build up the body of Christ, his Church.

Lay eucharistic ministers:

- help to give Communion at Mass
- take Communion to those who are sick or housebound
- offer a witness to the community by their service.

Questions to ponder and discuss

How do I serve God and others at present? Do I think of this as ministry?

What roles of service or ministry (liturgical and other) currently exist in my parish community? Who does this work?

2

Who can be a Lay Eucharistic Minister?

Most adult Roman Catholics, male and female, can become eucharistic ministers. We do not need special qualifications or to be especially pious. Lay ministers are, by definition, not ordained. We live with our family or alone; work; may have children. We have respect both for the Eucharist and for Christ's people. We belong to the community we are going to serve and are accepted there. We are able and willing to do what is asked of us.

> Most active Catholics can become eucharistic ministers. Ordinary people, who are willing to serve their parish family, are asked to give Communion to their sisters and brothers.

Although we may well feel drawn to this ministry and offer ourselves, it is good when fellow parishioners confirm this calling, either by saying something encouraging or recommending us to the parish clergy. This suggests that we have already shown many of the qualities required of a lay eucharistic minister. Probably the first thing people notice is that we are at Sunday Mass each week, join in the prayers and responses and receive Communion devoutly. The second is just as important: we have time for others. Without knowing it, we have passed the preliminary 'tests'.

Basic requirements

Eucharistic ministers must be Roman Catholics, confirmed believers in good standing with the Church and living according to the laws of the Church. Those who have become Catholic in adult life are as welcome as those brought up in Catholic families, though generally we give new Catholics time to grow familiar with our ways first. It is not appropriate for children to take on such responsibility, but many parishes suggest liturgical ministry to young adults (those who are 16 or over) immediately after confirmation.

It is important that eucharistic ministers have a basic awareness of what the Mass is about and express their understanding in active participation. We are not examined on our faith, but it will show through in worship, respect for the Blessed Sacrament and our everyday lives.

Social skills

Our faith is also expressed in the way in which we relate to others. Parishioners notice those who smile and say hello before Mass and who stay around to chat afterwards. They know who will offer a helping hand or a word of sympathy. They see who is respectful to poor and rich, old and young, women and men, every ethnic grouping.

When we look for possible eucharistic ministers, we often single out those who are thoughtful of others and interested in people. These social skills can be translated into a liturgical context when we welcome communicants at the altar, recognizing them as God's chosen, when we speak to them of mysteries and draw from them a response in faith, and when we share the holy gifts with them.

Already this may sound as if eucharistic ministers must be extraordinary people with very special gifts. In truth, without wanting to sound contradictory, we need people who do not stand out from the crowd. Eucharistic ministers are like everyone else in the parish; trying to live as Christians while coping with everything that life in the twenty-first century brings. We are not ready-made saints but disciples, learning as we go along, following Jesus. The only special thing about us is that we feel privileged to share the body and blood of Christ with our sisters and brothers; it is a wonder and source of joy for us.

You have seen lay eucharistic ministers at work in your own and other parishes. Make a list below of the things they do to make you feel welcome at the Lord's table.

At the end, write in anything that angers or upsets you about their ministry.

Why ask me?

Occasionally, the invitation to become a lay eucharistic minister comes as a surprise. We had never considered doing such a thing and our first impulse is to find excuses to say no: 'I'm too shy', 'I'll make a mistake with everyone watching', 'I don't have the time'. Most difficulties can be overcome if we are willing. We may just need to get used to the idea and pray about it.

Often a supportive friend encourages us to ask ourselves, 'Why not?' without applying pressure. However, if, after much thought, a person really does not feel it is for them, it is as well to say so. They may be more suited to a different ministry or take up the invitation in the future. Eucharistic ministers must want to serve their communities – that is what ministry means. Sometimes people feel that they do not have the confidence, but it comes with practice.

Lay eucharistic ministers do not need lots of spare time. Parishes try to arrange training sessions and occasional meetings to fit in with family routines and work commitments. Apart from these considerations, the only thing that is required is to make very sure we arrive in good time for the service at which we are to minister. Additionally, those ministers who have more free time may be willing also to take Communion to sick and housebound people.

It may seem strange to say that eucharistic ministers must be able to do the work. Surely there is nothing difficult about sharing out a dish of bread or passing a cup of wine back and forth? This is just the point. Nobody has to be excluded from ministry because of impaired hearing, mild learning difficulties or stiff joints. Some of us may need a handrail or ramp or a bit of help and understanding from fellow ministers, but, if we can do all that is necessary, safely and respectfully, we can minister.

Eucharistic ministers must:

- be baptized and confirmed Catholics
- participate in Sunday Mass each week and receive Communion
- understand what happens at Mass and why it is important
- be respectful of holy things
- try to live a Christian life
- be thoughtful of others, helpful and friendly
- have respect for people of every kind
- be accepted by the parish community
- be able to do the work and follow instructions
- take responsibility
- be willing to serve.

I am not worthy

To receive Communion implies that we are 'in communion' and have not committed any sin so grave as to cut us off from the Church community. At the same time, receiving Communion is a powerful way to heal our relationship with Christ and his people, which we may have damaged by our failings. As scripture tells us, we have all sinned and fallen short of God's glory (Romans 3:23) and so all eucharistic ministers rightly have a sense of unworthiness when they are asked to give the body and blood of Christ to others. In that case, we might well ask, who *is* worthy? The wonderful reality is that Christ has made us all worthy, through his blood. If we are good enough to eat and drink and receive Christ within ourselves (and the Church urges us to take Communion frequently, even daily), then we must be good enough to share his holy gifts with others.

It is clear, then, that becoming a eucharistic minister is not a reward for special holiness and we should be wary of portraying ourselves as in some way better or more devout than others. Neither is this a way to make people with leadership roles in the parish or local community more visible, nor to flatter rich, powerful parishioners. It is unwise to invite people to become eucharistic ministers for the primary purpose of increasing their self-confidence, making them more committed or giving status to minority groups – though this may be an additional benefit. Equally, we should take care not to exclude anyone on such criteria.

New eucharistic ministers may wish to celebrate sacramental reconciliation (confession) before being commissioned if they have any worries at all. Most of us have events in our past that are best forgotten. However, if there is something that might cause grave offence in the parish if discovered, it is best to discuss it in confidence with the parish priest. Often what people may *think* is a serious impediment to liturgical ministry is of little importance in a community rooted in love, forgiveness and reconciliation.

Most adult Catholics who are trying to live their faith can become lay eucharistic ministers. Doubts are normal and obstacles can usually be overcome, if we are willing to serve. Taking on this responsibility brings great blessings.

Questions to ponder and discuss

What would prevent someone from becoming a eucharistic minister?

Why do/did I want to become a eucharistic minister?

3

Becoming a Lay Eucharistic Minister

When we allow our lives to become a journey of faith, we grow in courage and commitment. We watch others take on roles in the liturgy or other aspects of parish life and no longer think 'Rather them than me.' We know their names, have chatted at the school gates or worked together on a community project. They are neighbours, friends or family, they are people just like us and one day we may think 'I could do that too.'

It is a fortunate parish that has more than enough trained liturgical ministers. Most need, as a minimum, to replace those who have moved away or find they can no longer serve for some reason. Some decide that they need to train quite a few more if they are to celebrate well.

In some parishes there is an open appeal or an occasional introductory session. (This may not bring in many suitable volunteers, but it is a useful way to keep the work of lay liturgical ministers in the minds of parishioners.) Other parishes rely on the clergy to make personal contact or ask current lay ministers to suggest possible candidates. Whichever way is used, our parish invites us to think about liturgical ministry and, specifically, to consider becoming a eucharistic minister. When the time is right, we stop murmuring 'No way' and say instead 'Perhaps.'

Finding out more

Almost certainly, our next step is to find out more. Probably we start by watching eucharistic ministers with far greater attention than ever before. We see that there is a firm shape to the ministry, that people work as a team and take individual responsibility for some tasks. If we are brave, we get chatting to them to find out what it's like. Human beings are naturally cautious and most parishes would rather we took our time to think and pray about ministry than leap in, only to change our minds after a month or two.

Parishes may offer a more structured way to learn a bit more about being a eucharistic minister. Perhaps a day of study and recollection is arranged for a group or an outside speaker is invited or a meeting with current ministers is arranged, as they are just the people to answer our questions. Often, what we think are insurmountable difficulties just melt away as soon as we mention them. Others have come this way before us and smoothed the path for those who follow. In addition, it can be wonderfully consoling to find that the majority of current ministers do not have degrees in theology, nor haloes, and that they started out as apprehensive as we are now.

Acceptance

After a little more thought and a lot more prayer, our 'Perhaps' will hopefully become a 'Yes', even if it is a tentative one. This is an interesting moment because it implies acceptance on both sides. The new minister is willing to serve their community, and the community agrees to receive their service. The bond between the individual and the assembly of worshippers is strengthened. As the apostle Paul explained, we are Christ's body and each of us has a part to play in the whole (1 Corinthians 12:27).

A period of training will follow. This combines talks and discussions with practical sessions, always accompanied by prayer, but can be as formal or informal as we choose. In smaller parishes, training may well be done by the parish priest and existing eucharistic ministers; larger ones may have a liturgy coordinator or bring in a guest speaker. In the talks, it is helpful to explore the theme of ministry, learn more about the Mass and understand the Church's teaching on the Eucharist. Don't worry, there are no exams to pass – the aim is to give new ministers confidence and deepen our spiritual lives further. We may learn new ways of praying or go further in ways that are already familiar. Almost certainly, we will gain a new appreciation of liturgical prayer.

The person who has been appointed to be an extraordinary minister of Holy Communion is necessarily to be duly instructed and should distinguish himself by his Christian life, faith and morals. Let him strive to be worthy of this great office; let him cultivate devotion to the Holy Eucharist and show himself as an example to the other faithful by his piety and reverence for this most holy Sacrament.

Immensae Caritatis, 1973

Learning what to do

Practical training is best done in your church or other place where you will usually serve as a eucharistic minister and with the cloths and vessels normally used. The first task is to become familiar with the tools of our ministry, so we need to handle chalices, purificators and suchlike. In this way we can learn to use them respectfully and confidently. We also need to overcome any diffidence about approaching the altar, remembering that we are the people Christ calls to his table. To practise giving Communion, unconsecrated hosts are used, with plain water in the chalice, so that we can repeat the actions as often as we need until we are comfortable with them.

As well as the actions of sharing the host and wine, practical training should cover associated tasks, such as breaking a host cleanly with one hand. If a pouring chalice or flagon contains the wine during the eucharistic prayer, ministers need to practise transferring it to smaller chalices without spilling any of the contents, judging the quantities so that they are filled equally. Even wiping and turning the chalice is a learned skill and our first attempts are often awkward.

New ministers should be taken to the sacristy and shown where the sacred vessels and linens are stored, as well as where to put used cloths for laundering. One day, we may need to fetch an extra purificator or some other item during Mass and we need to be able to find them quickly. It is helpful to be told the proper names for some items and the differences between similar ones, though it is not necessary to know every last detail about them. As we grow into the ministry, we will learn more, but meanwhile, there is a glossary at the back of the book to help.

Anything that there might be a knack to should be tried out in practice sessions. Lids and stoppers may pull straight off or need to be turned. Pyxes (small containers in which consecrated hosts are kept to take to the sick and housebound) often have particularly tight closures. Equally, doors, gates and so on open and are held shut in various ways. Some tabernacles have troublesome locks and we need to learn to turn them smoothly. A few people, at least, should also know where the tabernacle key is kept in case of an emergency. Such items can cause much embarrassment and the last thing a new minister needs is to be fighting with something a bit tricky in the middle of Mass.

Practise everything

In general, we learn best when we first talk about what to do, then watch someone else do it and finally try it for ourselves. Although new ministers will have watched others, sometimes for many years, it is still helpful to be taken through the process of approaching the altar, reverencing it and beginning our work. We need to be shown where to stand and even, perhaps, how to walk. This sounds strange, but it can be distracting if we make sudden movements or cross behind the priest. We do not want to get in his way, either. Some people worry about walking down steps carrying a chalice until they have practised it. Others use visual references to position themselves correctly to give Communion. They need to stand on the right spot themselves, not just see someone else there.

We also need to go through the post-Communion routine. The best practice is not to return to the altar at all, but to consume all that remains and take the empty vessels and cloths directly to the small credence table. These items will be washed thoroughly after Mass, but, immediately after Communion, the vessels are rinsed with a little water, which is then drunk. Sometimes, consecrated hosts that remain are not consumed but placed in the tabernacle for the sick or future Communion services.

Becoming more skilled

Good ministers respond to people's needs in subtle ways that are impossible to catalogue. They anticipate difficulties. They may bend down, the better to give Communion to a child, or tactfully support the chalice for someone who is frail. Often it looks instinctive, yet such non-verbal skills of communication seem to be passed on among ministers. They are hard to teach formally, which is why we need to watch fellow ministers at work and note these personal touches. It is these tiny things that make the difference between a routine Communion and a true encounter with Christ and his body.

Mostly, the skills we learn are transferable – Communion is given in a similar way wherever we go – but each community has its own customs and traditions. Often these reflect the physical characteristics of the worship space and the sensibilities of the people there. So, although this book can give a general description of the work of a eucharistic minister, we will certainly find that one or two things are done differently in our own community. Eventually, we may even want to suggest further tiny adaptations that would make Communion more prayerful and more practicable in our church.

Rite of commissioning

When our training has been completed and if all is well, we are commissioned as lay eucharistic minister for our specific community. Commissioning is a way of mandating us and authorizing our ministry, so it is most appropriately done when the community we will serve is assembled for worship, preferably at Sunday Mass.

The short rite asks us to declare publicly our willingness to minister. It also invites the people to accept and welcome us and encourages them to pray for us.

All that then remains is for us to join the rota. Kindly rota-makers team new ministers with more experienced ones for a while, so that there is someone to watch over us as we grow in confidence. We may hope that, one day, we will give the same kind of support to a newly commissioned minister ourselves. Thus, our Christian journey continues. We will have deepened our faith and grown stronger in our commitment both to Christ and to his people. We have learnt that to say 'yes' to God leads to joy and a growing trust in him.

The journey of becoming a eucharistic minister includes talks and discussion, demonstrations and practical training. Above all, it requires much prayer.

We learn more about ministry, the Mass and the Church's teaching on the Eucharist.

The preparation both gives us confidence and deepens our spiritual lives so that we can joyfully offer ourselves to serve our communities.

Questions to ponder and discuss

How did you agree to become a eucharistic minister?

How would you choose and invite other people to the ministry?

If your community had unlimited time and resources, what would be the ideal way to train new eucharistic ministers?

Are any of these ideas achievable with the resources that you have?

4

An Ancient Privilege Restored

Many Catholics assume that lay eucharistic ministers are a very new introduction in the history of the Church. Perhaps this is true of the work we now do and current understanding of ministry, but the action of lay people giving Communion to themselves and others dates back to earliest times. After many centuries, the customs of the holy men and women who have gone before us are being restored to us.

The early centuries

After the Last Supper, the earliest accounts of eucharistic celebrations are probably in the Acts of the Apostles. In Jewish tradition, religious rituals, including memorials and thanksgivings, were often celebrated as full meals at home. The 'ministers' were family and friends. The first Christians inherited this idea, which may seem strange to us, for although we call the Eucharist a meal, we now only share token amounts of bread and wine. Paul's familiar complaint about the Christians of Corinth is not the abundance of food and drink that there was when they gathered, but that they did not share it. Some got drunk, while others went hungry, and this is not what the Lord's Supper should be (1 Corinthians 10:16–17; 11:20–34).

The New Testament letters give us tantalizing glimpses of the development of eucharistic liturgy among the first Christian communities. It seems that, fairly soon, there was a division between the full community meal and the ritual meal of shared bread and wine. Perhaps abuse like that at Corinth was all too common. The separation of community supper and ritual meal would also make it possible to have the eucharistic liturgy in the morning. (Of course, in later centuries, when there was a strict eucharistic fast from midnight, morning Mass became the norm.)

Many early writings on the Eucharist begin 'On the first day of the week'. It seems that Christian communities had settled into a routine of praying three times each day and celebrating the Lord's Supper every Sunday. A small story in Acts (20:7–12) tells us of a community that met on Saturday evening for the breaking of bread. (Of course, the 'first day of the week' is Sunday, but in Jewish and in early Christian thought, the day begins at sunset and we too celebrate the first Mass of Sunday on Saturday evening.) First, Paul preached long into the night – so long that at least one of those present fell asleep. Only then did they have the 'breaking of bread' together, continuing to eat and talk until dawn. It is probable that the pattern of teaching followed by a eucharistic rite was already established. For a century and more, Sunday would remain the only day for this kind of celebration.

The first good description of the Sunday Eucharist was written in Rome by Justin in about the year 150. In general form, it is indistinguishable from the Mass we celebrate today – there is even a collection! Justin writes of 'the one who presides' making a lengthy prayer of thanksgiving over the gifts, to which the people assent with 'Amen'. Then deacons distribute the bread and wine to all present and take a share to those who are absent. (We may assume that absentees include both the sick and those who were working, which raises an interesting possibility for our time.) This is the first evidence for Communion being given to those who are not physically present at the eucharistic liturgy. It is carried to them by deacons rather than lay people because the community has these servants of the bishop, chosen for liturgical and pastoral ministry.

A couple of generations later, though, we find matters have developed fast in Rome. The *Apostolic Tradition* (c. 215) offers a series of admonitions that only make sense if we assume that lay people took home the eucharistic bread from the Sunday celebration and kept it in their houses so as to give themselves daily Communion during the week. They were told to keep it safe and receive it worthily, preferably before they ate anything else, because it was the body of Christ. Other texts insisted that the dying were not to be deprived of *viaticum* (a last Communion) and stories tell of children being used as messengers to fetch the eucharistic bread for them. During these centuries, eucharistic worship was unknown. Christians were in no way disrespectful, but it was the act of sharing Communion that they venerated, not the reserved bread.

However, in North Africa there were already eucharistic liturgies on days other than Sunday – mostly on the fast days of Wednesday and Friday. This raised another problem: receiving Communion broke the fast, yet how could people gather for the Eucharist without receiving Communion? They simply carried it home with them so that it would be the first food they would eat to break their fast at sunset.

Gradually the practice of eucharistic celebrations on days other than Sunday spread, both throughout the Christian world and to all the days of the week. In theory, it was no longer necessary for lay people to keep the Eucharist at home or give themselves Communion. Indeed, it was far more desirable that they should gather together for worship than follow a private ritual. In practice, lay people did not easily give up their privilege. From the fourth to the eighth centuries, the custom gradually died out, though the surviving number of objections and condemnations of the practice suggest a solid core of resistance. Even Bede comments on it in the *Historia Ecclesiastica* (IV, 24).

The Middle Ages

By the ninth century, we begin to see detailed rites for the Communion of the sick for the first time. They are often accompanied by notes insisting that lay people should not take Communion to the sick (which, again, suggests it was still common practice). The ritual is reserved to priests alone, though it is unclear whether this is because Communion often follows penitential and anointing rites or because the priests are perceived to be failing in their pastoral care.

At the same time, other things were happening in the Church that would lead to a very different understanding of the Eucharist. Once Christianity became an official religion in the fourth century, the number of people seeking baptism increased rapidly. There were moves towards greater organization and regulation, as well as an adoption of ceremonial to dignify the Church's place in society. Legislation that had been intended simply to preserve sound doctrine and prevent abuse began a slow, slow process of distancing lay people from the Eucharist. Social change continued the work over the following centuries. Communion was no longer given in the hand (the only way it had been given previously) but in the mouth. Also, people came to Communion less often, the chalice was withheld, the people were given Communion after (not during) Mass, altars were screened and women forbidden to approach. A law had to be introduced to force lay people to receive Communion at least once a year.

A more dangerous transition was from symbol to allegory. The liturgy is essentially symbolic. That is, simple words and actions lead us into a complex relationship with the God who is beyond human comprehension and yet richly reveals himself to us. Symbols are ambiguous, offering many meanings and drawing us into new ways of thinking, believing and acting. Allegory, on the other hand, attempts to explain away liturgy or neatly tie it down to a single meaning. For example, the priest's necessary washing of hands is reinvented as a rite of spiritual purification or, even more extreme, the dropping of a fragment of the host into the chalice is interpreted as the return of Christ's soul to his body. Allegory makes us passive spectators; we no longer actively search for meaning.

Worship of the Eucharist

By the high Middle Ages, eucharistic liturgy was overwhelmed by eucharistic devotion. Exaggerated and inappropriate respect was shown to the consecrated host, while the Communion of the faithful was neglected. The people were imbued with a sense of sinfulness and there were many folk tales of God's wrath being unleashed on those who received Communion unworthily. The desire to share Communion was replaced by a desire to gaze on the host – often for extended periods. There are reports of lay people rushing from altar to altar to catch the elevation of the host at each Mass and shouting 'longer' to the priest when he put the host down to continue the eucharistic liturgy. We now call this strange practice 'ocular Communion' because the original purpose of the elevation (an invitation to Communion) had been forgotten and it had become an opportunity for private adoration. It is easy to see how eucharistic processions, the custom of praying at the place where the consecrated host was reserved (tabernacles only began to appear in the thirteenth century), exposition outside of Mass and Benediction, all developed at this time. They were responses to an unnatural situation. The people's longing for Communion, denied its fulfilment, was expressed instead as worship of the Blessed Sacrament.

It is hard to believe now, but the Council of Trent in the sixteenth century tried to reform the Church in the same way that Vatican II did in our own time. It was unfortunate that there was another Reformation underway at the time. The new liturgy books acknowledged the Council's desire to restore ancient customs (including the faithful receiving sacramental Communion at every Mass), but they also set out to defend Catholic worship from Protestant ideas. Those rites continued in use for some 400 years, with minimal changes, until Vatican II ordered that the liturgical books be revised again. No wonder that when today's Catholics talk about the past, it is usually Tridentine rites that they have in mind.

Modern reforms

This chapter might seem rather dull to those with little interest in history, while to those who have made a study of liturgy, it will seem a gross simplification of complex developments. However, it may explain why, when the Church renews herself in every age, she does not forever invent new ideas and practices, but brings forth from her storehouse treasures that will speak to the needs and sensitivities of the present.

The impetus that led to Vatican II had begun early in the twentieth century, with fresh encouragement to receive frequent, even daily, Communion. Even the most unworthy sinner could go to confession on Saturday and Communion on Sunday. The traditional order of sacramental initiation was reversed, with children as young as seven years old being invited to Communion. After the Council, the time was right to give back to lay people the active participation in the liturgy that they had once enjoyed and, among much else, remind them of their ancient right to give Communion to others. The first Council document was on the liturgy (*Sacrosanctum Concilium*, 1963). We now take for granted all that was restored then: liturgy in our own language; short, clear rites; Communion under both kinds; Sunday Mass on Saturday evening, and much else.

A good proportion of the official documents on the liturgy published since Vatican II are concerned with practical matters such as the right way to celebrate Mass. However, there are also passages that attempt to explain the changes and relate them to the earlier history of the Church. These documents are rather dry, so we tend to read only fragments, quoted in books like this, but one sentence is so important, and so often reported, that we know it almost by heart:

Liturgy is the summit toward which the activity of the Church is directed; it is also the fount from which all her power flows.

Sacrosanctum Concilium, 10

The liturgy is not simply Mass for an hour on Sundays before we get on with 'real' life. It is the means by which we offer all we do and all we are to God, and receive from him everything we need for our spiritual, physical and communal wellbeing and growth. We cannot be onlookers; it demands full and active participation. We are most fully human when we allow the liturgy to be the goal of all our striving and the source of all our strength.

The Eucharist developed from Jewish ritual meals, in which all present were active participants.

In the early centuries of the Church, Christians respected the eucharistic bread as the body of Christ and symbol of shared Communion. They did not worship it. Lay people gave Communion to themselves and others.

In the following centuries, the people were distanced from active participation in the liturgy. Eucharistic devotion and adoration of the Blessed Sacrament replaced frequent Communion.

Vatican II returned to the older forms of the liturgy and restored the rights and privileges of lay people.

Questions to ponder and discuss

Vatican II desired full and active participation in the liturgy for all the faithful. Do you think this has been achieved?

Is the Church right to place so much reliance on the rites and customs of past centuries? Should future generations be free to invent new rituals for their own time?

5

The Mass as Sacrifice, Meal and Communion

The Mass as sacrifice

We do not need to look any further than our eucharistic prayers to understand the Mass as sacrifice. Each one explicitly reminds us of the Passion and death of the Lord, and the words 'sacrifice' and 'offering' run through them as a constant theme. What kind of sacrifice, though, and whose?

The Mass is not an Old Testament ritual – we don't kill an animal or burn our offerings on the altar so that the sweet smell rises to heaven. The Eucharistic Prayer 1 says this: 'Through him [Jesus Christ] we ask you to accept and bless these gifts we offer you in sacrifice' and 'We offer you this sacrifice of praise for ourselves and those who are dear to us.'

It should be absolutely clear that we cannot, and need not, repeat Christ's offering of himself for our salvation. He has completed that work and we, in any case, cannot save ourselves. It is slightly confusing that we speak of the Mass as a memorial. In the liturgy, we do not simply remember past events, but make them powerfully present here and now. We do not look back on Christ's death and resurrection, but participate in it. For the eternal God, there is no past or future; everything is now. In the liturgy, we enter into God's timelessness.

Liturgical language is deliberately imprecise. Like an icon, it aims to lead us into the mystery. The classic form of a eucharistic prayer is, 'Remembering . . . we offer . . . and we pray . . .'. All we have to offer materially is bread and wine, yet, by remembering in this special way, they are imbued with meanings. We offer a sacrifice of praise. We are not giving God lip-service; our true worship is a sign of our commitment, our self-giving.

The Eucharist is not a re-enactment of the sacrifice of Calvary.

It is a 'sacrifice of praise' by which we share in Christ's saving work and give ourselves to God's service.

The Mass as meal

It seems to have come as a surprise to many people when, in the last part of the twentieth century, we started talking about the Mass as meal. Yet, in the early centuries of Christianity, this was self-evident. When the first believers gathered for the Lord's Supper, they ate together as Jesus and his disciples had done at the Last Supper. 'Do this in memory of me' had a generous interpretation because it was 'as they were eating' that Jesus had taken bread and blessed it and given it to his friends.

In part, this was because the first Christians were familiar with the Jewish customs of memorial meals and thanksgiving meals. They simply adapted what they knew to develop their own forms of worship – Jesus had not left them a text to follow. However, as the Church spread beyond Palestine, there was a gradual separation of the Eucharist and fellowship meal. Eventually the latter slipped out of regular use. Although there was still bread and wine at Mass, the meal aspect was increasingly forgotten, not least because lay people stopped receiving Communion frequently. Indeed, it was popularly thought to be sacrilegious to bite or chew the host – a view that lasted well into the twentieth century.

One of the most significant liturgical changes in our time has been the introduction of prayers over the gifts ('Blessed are you, Lord, God of all creation . . .') based on Jewish table blessings that are still in use today. We have rightly begun to restore the balance and teach that the Mass is meal as well as sacrifice. It is not finished until all the faithful have done as Jesus commanded, have eaten and drunk. We cannot offer our gifts as a sacrifice of praise unless we are willing to receive them back as our spiritual food.

The Mass as meal also builds community – one bread is broken as food for us all and we share one cup. To further emphasize this, the altar table is usually now freestanding. We have a real sense of gathering around it and thus gathering around Christ.

Curiously, as we are rediscovering the symbolism and power of the eucharistic meal, society is forgetting the importance of family meals. Those preparing children for Communion report that they are not learning how to share a meal around a table at home. Snacking, TV meals, eating at different times, eating different foods and so on are the norms. It means that we have to work harder at the experience of sharing a meal and investing it with meaning. The Lord's Supper is what binds us together as the Church. Through it, we become one body in Christ.

> The Mass is a ritual meal. By sharing one bread and one cup, we proclaim that we are one community, gathered as Christ's body.

The eucharistic prayers

The word 'eucharist' means thanksgiving. All the eucharistic prayers essentially just give thanks, though this is woven through with praise and offering. We give thanks for creation and salvation – the two great events that define and order our relationship with God. Usually in the eucharistic prayers we remind ourselves just how much we have to be thankful for by referring to significant moments in the Old Testament and the life of Jesus. We always tell of his Passion, death, resurrection and ascension to glory.

'Eucharist' means thanksgiving.

We also repeat the story of the Last Supper and Jesus' command, 'Do this in memory of me' (the Words of Institution), as our mandate for celebrating the Eucharist. This passage is familiarly called the consecration, though it is more helpful to think of the whole eucharistic prayer as consecratory as it is not sufficient to say these words alone. The priest must repeat the chosen eucharistic prayer in full for a valid Mass. Giving thanks and praise are integral parts of the eucharistic mystery.

In the process of giving thanks, God's power is joined to our human desire, and the common bread and wine become the body and blood of the Lord. We have to accept this by faith. The gifts still look like the bread and wine we brought to the altar minutes before. When we receive them in Communion, they still feel and smell and taste like bread and wine. Our senses tell us nothing has changed, but our active participation in the liturgy assures us that our senses have been deceived and these are truly the body and blood of Christ. God is faithful, he does not cheat us; he does as he has promised.

The celebrating people are in fact the people of God, purchased by the blood of Christ, convened by their Lord, nourished by his word, a people called to lay before God the entreaties of all humanity. They are a people who give thanks to God for the mystery of salvation in Christ by offering his sacrifice; a people who grow together in unity by being united with his Body and Blood; a people, holy by origin, who continually grow in holiness by active, conscious and fruitful participation in the eucharistic mystery.

General Instruction on the Roman Missal, 1970, Foreword 5

Bread of life, blood of the covenant

We need to understand fully what these gifts mean for us. They are not two parts of a whole, 'flesh and blood', which is why Communion is complete even if we can only receive the bread alone or the cup alone. When Jesus said, 'This is my body, given for you', he was not talking about a Shakespearian pound of flesh but his whole life, living in service to humanity and dying that we might live. The cup, too, is 'The blood of the new and everlasting covenant, shed for all people so that sins may be forgiven.' The apostles would have understood this far better than we do. God had made a solemn agreement with the Jewish people ('I will be your God, you will be my people'), which was sealed with the blood of sacrificial animals. That covenant was broken and renewed more than once. The new covenant, made in Christ's blood, is forever and for all peoples. The relationship, sealed with blood, is one of forgiveness.

There is a little more to add. Jesus told us, 'My flesh is real food and my blood is real drink' (John 6:55, NJB). The eucharistic bread and wine are given to heal and nourish and sustain us. For us, bread is an everyday staple, an essential food. It has even been called the staff of life. Wine usually brings a lifting of spirits, a feeling of celebration. In moderate quantities, it is good for our health and wellbeing.

A paschal meal

Bread and wine are paired in many religious rituals, not least in the Jewish Passover meal (which, by some Gospel accounts, was the setting for the Last Supper). The Passover rite speaks of the 'bread of affliction, bread of the poor', but also 'bread of freedom'. During it, God's promises to his people are recalled with cups of wine.

This annual meal service commemorates the deliverance of the Israelites from bondage in Egypt. In wider terms, it is about the making of a people and their individual and collective journey from the darkness of sin to light and freedom in the land of promise. An essential element is that the story is passed on to children, who must claim it for themselves: 'I was a slave in Egypt; the Lord redeemed me too.'

The Gospels certainly intend us to read the accounts of the Last Supper, and Jesus' Passion and death, against this backdrop. Through the ages, artists have depicted Jesus as the Lamb of God – a direct reference to the Passover story – and this is how we address him at Mass at the breaking of the bread in preparation for Communion. Historically, Christians have rarely shown much appreciation of the Jewish roots of our faith, but our spiritual lives will be greatly enriched if we do understand better how what we do and say in the liturgy draws on the Jewish scriptures and Jewish worship.

Christ's presence

At Mass, Christ is not only present in the consecrated bread and wine. He is also powerfully present in the Christian community gathered for worship. We are the body of Christ. Christ is present in the word of God proclaimed to us in the readings and, indeed, we call him the Word of God. Often, now, we talk about the Mass as feeding at two tables as the table of the word also offers us a rich banquet. Christ is present, too, in a special way through the ministry of the priest who presides at the liturgy.

When we gather for Sunday Eucharist, we are not like any other assembly of people. We try to express the bonds that unite us through metaphor and poetry. The *Didache*, which contains the earliest written text of a eucharistic prayer (possibly AD70), sees us as grains of wheat, gathered from many hills, baked together into one bread. Jesus himself said, 'I am the vine, you are the branches.' Paul described us as the many parts that make up one single body, with Christ as the head. All of these express an organic unity that identifies us with our Saviour. We were baptized in him and cannot unwillingly be separated from him, yet we are most visibly one in him when we celebrate the Eucharist together.

The presiding priest is a visible expression of Christ's presence, especially when he re-presents Christ's words and actions at the Last Supper. Though called and ordained for this very special ministry, the priest is as human as we are. He stands as 'first among equals' to lead the community in worship. We are always aware that Jesus is the true High Priest. It is he who takes our prayers and offerings to the Father and he who gives them back to us, transformed. Our baptismal anointing makes us all prophets, priests and kings and this priesthood of all believers is very precious to us. It makes us like Christ, ministers and servants. Ordained priests and bishops have a distinctive ministry. To them is given power to act in the person of Christ. They do so within, and with the assent of, the Christian community. Through their ministry we meet Christ in the sacraments.

At Mass, Christ is present in the:
- word we share
- consecrated bread and wine
- gathered community
- priest who presides at our liturgy.

The Church as communion

Communion can mean both sharing and participation. Though we Catholics usually talk about 'giving Communion' or 'receiving Communion', other Christians use the word 'communicate'. It suggests a connectedness and also reminds us of passing on non-verbal messages. A third word we often link with these two is 'unity'. In sharing Communion, we are bound together and made one with each other and with our God. In this way we are a communion, the Church is a communion.

When the eucharistic minister says to us, 'The body of Christ' and we say 'Amen' (which means 'Yes, so be it'), we are giving assent in two distinct ways. We make a profession of faith that the food we receive is not common bread, but Christ himself. We also say yes to the proposition that *we* are Christ's body. Augustine frequently made this point to his community. He said to them, 'There you are on the altar and there you are in the chalice' (Sermon 229). He explained this further in Sermon 272, referring to Paul and saying, 'You are the body of Christ and his members. It is your mystery which is set forth on the Lord's table; it is your own mystery that you receive. You say "Amen" to what you are, and in saying "Amen" you subscribe to it. For you hear the words "the body of Christ", and you answer "Amen". Be members of the body of Christ, then, so that your "Amen" might be authentic.'

> We say Amen to what we are.
>
> *Cf. Augustine, Sermon 272*

When we say amen to the body and blood of Christ, we give joyous assent to our unity with one another and with our Head. Also, though, we are assenting to the proposition that we are to be, like him, bread broken and wine poured out for others. In other words, we give ourselves to this community of faith unconditionally; we give our whole lives to others. Humanly, we might prefer to turn back or to give only to a limited extent. The Eucharist challenges us to be more like Christ and offers us the strength to do so.

The community that celebrates

The reserved sacrament (the consecrated bread kept in the tabernacle for future use) always refers back to the community that gathered to celebrate the Eucharist. When we give Communion to the sick, we both bring them spiritual food and assure them that they remain part of the eucharistic community. They are remembered in the thanksgiving prayer and a share of Christ's gifts is reserved for them. Similarly, eucharistic worship and personal devotions are never a private, individual matter. We are able to contemplate the Blessed Sacrament only because the eucharistic community made provision for this too. Those people's work of prayer and thanksgiving is represented in the host. They surround us, support us and share in our worship as we are able to share in theirs.

The Eucharist is the crown of our worship and the heart of our Christian lives. Full and active participation is not solely, or even primarily, a matter of joining in the prayers and actions by rote. It requires an engagement of the mind and spirit, a willingness to become participants in the mystery of faith, both liturgically and in every aspect of our lives. Every Christian is called to this, most especially ministers of the Eucharist, the servants at the eucharistic liturgy. This is a cause of joy for us, not a worry. Our Lord has done all the hard work for us, borne the pain, and now we are invited to share in his victory feast.

The Mass is a sacrifice, a meal and a thanksgiving. In the Eucharist, we enter into the mystery of salvation. In Communion, we receive the body and blood of the Lord by faith, in the form of bread and wine, and we recognize ourselves as being the body of Christ.

Questions to ponder and discuss

The Mass is sacrifice and meal. How can it be both?

What do we give assent to when we say 'Amen' at Communion?

What does Augustine mean by 'We say Amen to what we are'?

6

Practical Training 1:
Communion During Mass

Each eucharistic community shares Communion in a slightly different way. The ideas presented in this chapter are standard methods of good practice. Every eucharistic ministers' group or liturgy committee should adapt them to suit their own needs. A table is provided at the end of the chapter to help all involved remember what has been agreed. It is important that everyone understands what needs to be done and why, rather than simply following instructions. This makes it easier to adapt to different situations and gives the necessary confidence to deal with any unusual events.

This chapter assumes that your community always offers Communion under both kinds at Mass or is training more ministers so that you can do so. If this is not the case, ask what prevents it.

Many small differences

Some variations will be dictated by the shape, size and physical characteristics of the church or other space where Communion is given. Perhaps there is an unusual seating arrangement or very little space around the altar. Some historic churches still have altar rails, at which the people kneel for Communion.

It can be useful to look at what happens at present. Is there a dignified procession to Communion or confusion about where to go? Do the people bunch in certain places? Can wheelchair users get to Communion?

Communities also have greater or lesser requirements of their eucharistic ministers. Some will not only distribute the bread and wine, but also help with the breaking of bread, fill the chalices before Communion, take unused hosts to the tabernacle after Communion, put bread in a pyx for Communion of the sick and purify altar vessels. In part, Church law has not wholly synchronized with modern liturgical practice yet. For example, theoretically, lay people may handle the sacred vessels to give Communion, but not rinse them out afterwards. In practice, it seems sensible for the eucharistic ministers to do such tasks, and the Church is moving towards this position.

Other things that vary from place to place include the moment when ministers come to the altar, how they reverence it as they approach and when they themselves receive Communion. Some communities have a dress code for ministers (jeans and T-shirts may be thought too casual, for example) or ask them to wear a badge or other identifier. The role of the eucharistic minister may be amplified on special occasions, so, for instance, they may be given a prominent place in the Corpus Christi procession.

How many ministers?

There should always be sufficient ministers of Communion, ordained and lay, so that it can be given without haste and yet not be unduly prolonged. It is not acceptable to leave the precious blood on the altar or a table for people to help themselves; the chalice should be passed from hand to hand, from minister to recipient. Although no law prevents eucharistic ministers from giving themselves Communion, the better sign is for lay ministers to receive from someone else (either a priest or another lay minister) when possible. If nothing else, the graceful gestures of giving and receiving speak powerfully about our interdependence, our need both to serve and be served. At Mass, the priest-presider should always give Communion and the presence of concelebrants or deacons should be noted when deciding how many lay eucharistic ministers are required.

Not only do we need sufficient lay eucharistic ministers at each Mass, but we also need enough ministers to cover all Masses. In fact, we probably need three or four times that number so that people do not have to serve every Sunday. Lay people sometimes go away at weekends, they work, have visitors or family commitments. We cannot make ourselves available to minister on every Sunday of the year. It is also far better for the parish community to see many different people serving as eucharistic ministers than the same few every week.

The Communion procession

Usually it is preferable to give Communion from one position only and generally this is in front of the altar. In very large churches or difficult spaces, secondary Communion points may be set up for practical reasons. They should be clearly indicated and not cramped, so that people can still approach decorously. Ministers should not normally move through an assembly while giving Communion but stand still and allow others to approach them. Of course, it is acceptable for ministers to take Communion to someone with mobility difficulties, especially if this has been requested beforehand.

The normal ratio is two ministers with chalices for every one giving the host. As people receive the body of Christ first, these ministers will act as a focus for the Communion procession. The ministers with chalices then draw people onwards and into a circular flow back to their seats. It is better not to have people double back on themselves if it can be avoided, not least because the symbolism of the procession is lost. We can increase the sense of prayer and respect by making the route of the Communion procession predictable and serene.

Occasionally, the gentle flow such patterns create is broken by a communicant who wants to make some personal gesture of respect or to receive kneeling. A loving community should be able to accommodate such things. In fact, the Church recommends that we all make a sign of reverence before receiving the Blessed Sacrament, though we should do so in a way that does not disrupt the Communion procession (*Eucharisticum Mysterium*, 34). A bow as the person before us receives Communion would seem appropriate.

Here is a simple pattern.

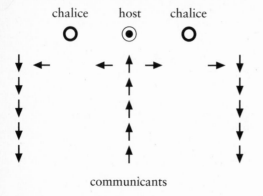

Here is a double pattern.

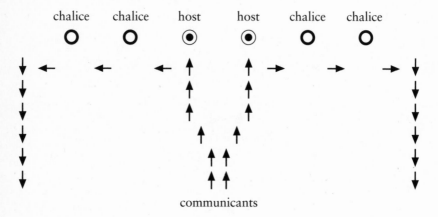

The route of the Communion procession should also allow anyone who does not wish to receive from the chalice to bypass it easily.

Truly Christ in form of bread and wine

Lay eucharistic ministers may distribute either the hosts or the wine. Both have been consecrated; both are truly the Lord. It is permissible to receive from the chalice alone, and this is as fully Communion as

receiving the bread alone. Priests sometimes feel that they must distribute the hosts, lest any who object to lay ministers are deprived of Communion. However, where the priest is never seen to give Communion
from the chalice, the people may think of it as being secondary in
importance, mere wine – blessed, perhaps, but still just wine.

Preparations for Communion

Eucharistic ministers normally approach the altar just before Communion, having been seated among the people up to that point. They
should avoid ostentation in their clothes and demeanour, so as not
to draw attention away from the altar and the gifts that will soon be
shared. For the same reason, they may prefer to approach from the
sides, rather than along the main axis of the church.

If they come to the altar in such an inconspicuous way, a sign of
respect may not be needed, but, if it is, a bow is preferable to genuflection. (Liturgically, the only genuflection *during* Mass is the priest's,
after the words of institution. It is also difficult to do properly.) Then,
unless the ministers have work to do in preparation for Communion,
they should stand still alongside the altar where they will not block
the people's view or be a distraction.

In most parishes in the UK, lay eucharistic ministers receive Communion after the priest but before the people, this being thought most
practical. In a few parishes, they receive at the same time as the
priest, which is a strong sign of community and a united ministry.
Periodically, liturgists suggest that the most powerful sign would be
for eucharistic ministers to receive Communion last, after the people,
as is appropriate for the servants at a feast. This is very practical,
too, as the remaining gifts could all be consumed.

It is recommended that Communion during Mass be given with
hosts consecrated at that Mass. There should be no need to use
previously consecrated hosts in normal circumstances and it should
certainly not be habitual to do so. However, eucharistic ministers
may have to bring the reserved sacrament from the tabernacle if there
are many extra communicants or place into it hosts consecrated for

Communion of the sick or for future services of word and Communion.

Hosts can always be broken into more pieces if required, but occasionally the chalices are empty before the end of Communion. There is no point at all in offering an empty cup. One possibility is for the minister to remain in place, with the purificator folded across the top of the chalice. However, the people do not always spot this or understand its significance. Alternatively, the minister can take the empty chalice to the credence table and wait beside it until Communion ends. This is more practical if other ministers still have full chalices. In general, though, it is a better sign of hospitality for eucharistic ministers to remain in place until everyone has received. In particular, those who give the host are likely to finish first and should wait while the last few communicants receive from the chalices.

It is usual to rinse the empty vessels with a little water (which is drunk by the minister) immediately after Communion. However, we should not make a great show of this or take very long over it, lest it seem an important part of Mass, which it is not. If the credence table is in full sight of the assembled community, it may be better to leave this task until the end of Mass rather than distract them from prayer. Once the vessels have been rinsed in this way, they should be given a proper wash in warm water after Mass.

Communion during Mass in your community may look something like this.

- The eucharistic ministers arrive in good time for Mass. They greet the presider or MC (so that their presence is noted) and fellow ministers.

- The lay ministers sit in the body of the church, with family or friends, but not in a group with other ministers. They take full part in the Mass.

- As the Sign of Peace ends, the eucharistic ministers approach the altar discreetly, briefly bowing their heads.

- If very large hosts are being used, one minister may be invited to help break them into smaller pieces.

- A minister may bring extra Communion dishes to the altar and/ or extra chalices and purificators, unless a server does this.

- If the wine has been consecrated in one large chalice or flagon, a minister may transfer it to smaller chalices suitable for Communion.

- If hosts from the tabernacle will be needed, one minister may bring the ciborium to the altar.

- If Communion will be taken to the sick from this Mass, the pyx or pyxes may be placed on the altar and filled.

- At the chosen time, the priest gives Communion to each of the eucharistic ministers or gives them the host and they receive the wine from a fellow minister.

- The priest gives or indicates the bread or wine to each minister. Those who will administer the chalice take a purificator also.

- Priest and ministers go to the points from which they give Communion.

- The ministers give Communion with respect and without haste. They make sure to give appropriate help to those with special needs.

- When the people have received Communion, priest and ministers take the empty vessels to the credence table.

- The priest or lay minister may consume any remaining hosts or place them in a ciborium and return it to the tabernacle.

- Any consecrated wine that remains in the chalices is normally drunk by the priest and ministers as it will not keep.

- Ministers may rinse Communion dishes and chalices with a little water, which is then drunk.

- The priest may call forward those who will take Communion to the sick and give them the filled pyxes now or he may defer this until after saying the Prayer after Communion.

- Ministers return discreetly to their seats.

- After Mass, eucharistic ministers may take responsibility for washing altar vessels thoroughly and putting them away safely.

Giving Communion

The bread

Allow the person receiving Communion to come to you, stop and look at you. Look at them with warmth. Take your time. With one hand, take a piece of the consecrated host (or an individual host) from the Communion dish in your other hand, raise it to chest height above the dish and say, clearly and audibly, still looking at them, 'The body of Christ'. Give the communicant time to respond, 'Amen'.

If the communicant has made a 'throne' with their cupped hands, place the host there gently but firmly. Wait while they transfer it to their mouth.

Otherwise, the communicant probably wants to receive on the tongue. Hold the host at the edge so that you can place a good part of it securely into the mouth without getting saliva on your fingers.

If it is not clear how a person wants to receive Communion, wait until they signal it more clearly either by stretching out their hands or opening their mouth wider.

Do not shift your eyes to the next person in line until the previous communicant has begun to move away.

A person who comes with their arms crossed on their chest has come for a blessing and should not be given Communion.

The wine

Most chalices have stems, and if the eucharistic minister holds the middle of this, most communicants instinctively grasp the bowl and the base, giving them a safe two-handed grip. Unless the communicant is very young or frail or shaky, hand over the chalice fully while the communicant drinks, then receive it back again. If there is good reason to keep a hand on the chalice, offer light support, but let the communicant control the tilting of the cup to drink.

Before starting to give Communion, open out the purificator and keep it in your free hand. As you wipe the chalice, use a different part of the cloth each time.

Allow the person receiving Communion to come to you, stop and look at you. Look at them with warmth. Take your time. Raise the chalice to chest height and say, clearly and audibly, still looking at them, 'The blood of Christ'. Give the communicant time to respond, 'Amen'.

Pass the chalice to them, make sure they have a firm grip and allow them to drink a little.

Receive back the chalice, taking it by the centre of the stem.

Do not make this person hurry away by shifting your eyes to the next person in line, but, when they do move on, wipe the edge of the chalice where they drank with a clean part of the purificator and give the chalice a quarter turn.

Occasionally a communicant will come with the host still in their hand. After the dialogue, lower the chalice so that they can dip the host into the wine. This is called intinction. It is normally used only when there is the likelihood of passing on an infection through the shared chalice.

A communicant may not wish to receive from the chalice and so will walk past. This is their choice; you do not need to know why. Remember that non-communicants who came up for a blessing will also bypass you.

Administering the blood of Christ seems to be the more difficult task, but eucharistic ministers quickly get into a rhythm and the wiping and turning becomes routine. New ministers are sometimes afraid to dirty the purificator, yet its sole purpose is to absorb any drips; it is laundered after every use. Another worry is that, while wiping the rim, they may accidentally dip the edge of the purificator into the precious blood. It rarely happens because chalices are not normally more than half full.

Eucharistic ministers are occasionally invited to give Communion at an informal house Mass and there may be very little space to move. In such circumstances, it may be necessary for the people to stay where they are and the eucharistic minister to go round to each of them in turn. This is far safer and more decorous than letting the people walk around in a confined space. Passing the Communion dish and chalice from hand to hand is not generally permitted – it is always preferable for the minister, lay or ordained, to give Communion to those assembled.

Questions to ponder and discuss

How does this compare with your actual experiences in your parish or community?

Do you do things in a different way or at a different time?

Are there things you do not do?

Take time to discuss as a group (or to think about) why your way of doing things better suits your community.

Are there alternatives you would like to try?

Look at the list of good and annoying practices you compiled in Chapter 2. Are there items you wish to incorporate into (or eliminate from) your ministry?

Giving Communion in my parish

Which Mass?	
Dress code	
Contact on arrival	
Moment to approach altar	
Route to take	
Gesture of respect?	
Stand behind or beside altar?	
Help with breaking of bread?	
Fill chalices?	
Bring ciborium from tabernacle?	
Lay ministers' Communion routine	
Where to stand to give Communion?	
Communicants with special needs	
Return to altar singly or together?	
Fill pyx for Communion of the sick?	
Take remaining hosts to tabernacle?	
Purify empty altar vessels?	
Wash vessels after Mass?	
Other things to remember	

This chart may be copied as required.

7

Practical Training 2:
Communion of the Sick

Taking Communion to those who are sick or housebound is very different from giving Communion in church. For one thing, the assembled community shrinks to very few people, sometimes just two. For another, the lay eucharistic minister also takes on the role of presider and leads the simple rite of Communion. The situation is often domestic and usually far more informal than a church service. The person receiving Communion may be seated in a comfortable armchair or resting in bed.

Hesitations

Not every lay eucharistic minister will want to take on this kind of service and not everyone will have the time to do it. Although it is fairly simple to learn the rite of Communion of the sick, there is a greater personal involvement. Some people are comfortable with this. Perhaps they already visit neighbours who are ill or housebound and see the giving of Communion as an extension of this ministry and an invitation to meet more housebound parishioners. Others don't quite know how to develop a one-to-one ministry in such a context.

Having free time is essential. The Communion of the sick cannot be hurried. We need to allow enough time in order to get to and from the home or hospital. We need time so as to ensure that a sick person knows why we have come and is comfortable before we begin. We need time to pace the rite, to make it prayerful without being unbearably long. We need time after Communion so that we do not have to rush away, but can talk with the sick person a little (not tiring them, though) or, if they are very ill, comfort their relatives and friends.

It is common to be a little afraid of illness, especially when we do not know the sick person very well. If we have no medical training, we might fear that we will do the wrong thing in an emergency, offer help inappropriately or not feel able to offer the kind of help that is needed. In reality, such worries are groundless. Anyone who is really ill will have an attendant (nurse, friend, family member) beside them during the Communion rite to take care of their personal needs.

More commonly, we are asked to take Communion to those who are not able to get out much, but can still look after themselves and do simple household tasks. These people are sometimes lonely, so the Communion minister's visit is a social as well as pastoral one. They hope for a chat afterwards and may offer tea. Again, not all of us feel wholly comfortable making conversation with someone we don't know too well. Of course, we may be agreeably surprised when an older person starts talking about their interests and their past.

Additional skills needed

If we choose to take Communion to sick or housebound people, it is helpful to have, or learn, some additional skills.

Presiding at this liturgy needs a special kind of leadership, a respectful authority that confidently directs the worship, while encouraging others to take full part. We are, of course, prayerful people, and that is the key to helping others become powerfully aware of Christ's presence. We need to speak clearly, read fluently and not be shy about praying aloud or keeping silence. It helps if we can quickly adjust our movements and gestures to unfamiliar spaces, often small and cluttered ones, and are equally responsive to another person's sensitivities. Good social skills are vital in this more intimate situation as we are entering someone's home or hospital room as their guest, by their or their family's invitation. Yet, in terms of the rite, we act as host, bringing the body of Christ and representing the community, the body of Christ, that shared the Lord's Supper and provided this spiritual food.

Shorter rite or fuller one?

The rite of Communion of the sick has two general forms. For someone who is quite ill, we use a brief rite that will not tire them too much. It expects limited or no response from the person. Communion may even be given as a drop of consecrated wine on the tongue if swallowing is difficult.

The Eucharist is sometimes thought to bring healing, and it does, if only by offering spiritual comfort and calming fears. Most people are expected to recover from their illness; some will not. When death is close, Communion may be the last food they receive. It is given a special name: *viaticum* – food to sustain them on their final journey to eternal life. Often a priest will give *viaticum*, not because the ministry is reserved to him, but because he celebrates the sacraments of reconciliation and the anointing of the sick at the same visit. It seems likely that lay ministers will have the privilege of giving *viaticum* more often in future, and even staying on a little longer to read the prayers for the dying.

Communion of the housebound, on the other hand, is not wholly about sickness and healing. Chronic illness or old age may impair mobility, but even physically healthy people can have difficulty getting to church. Mental illness and behavioural problems sometimes lead to feelings of social exclusion. Carers, too, often rely on the kindness and availability of friends to get a little time to themselves and Sunday morning may not be offered. Those who need Communion at home may be of any age. Sometimes it will be necessary for just a few weeks, but people in such situations often have regular visits from ministers of Communion over many years and will be actively involved in the preparations and celebration. Depending on the person's health and wishes, the readings of the previous Sunday and some of the Mass prayers may be shared; there can be formal or spontaneous intercessions and even a hymn or two. It is a joint enterprise, with the housebound person contributing much and even giving a lead.

Gathering a community of prayer

Whether we visit someone who is quite ill or merely unable to go out, family and friends who are present are encouraged to take full part in the Communion rite as a gathering of the Christian community in prayer. They can make the responses and may also be willing to share a scripture reading or pray spontaneously. Catholics are invited to receive Communion with the sick person. However, the eucharistic minister needs to present this sensitively. Sometimes family members are a bit shy and self-conscious in an unfamiliar situation and feel that they would not know what to do. They may not have been to Mass for a long time or think that they need first to confess their sins. As a sign of unity with the parish community, the eucharistic minister may choose to receive Communion too.

These days, Catholics often have relatives or close friends who are of other faiths. We should explain that our prayer will be Christ-centred and be welcoming if they choose to stay and pray in their own way.

Sometimes we can gather a small community for a Communion service, such as when a number of Catholics live in a residential home or sheltered accommodation. If it is practicable, it is always preferable to do this rather than bring Communion to each one individually. It helps to form and support the group and makes the gathering seem more of a celebration. People may be more willing to sing and actively take part in other ways, especially if one or two Catholic members of staff are present, too. It is often possible to reserve a small lounge or meeting space and even to display a cross or other symbol at the gathering.

Other needs of sick and housebound people

Housebound people often expect Communion to be a social event, too, which is understandable. Tea and a chat afterwards are fine, for a short time, but the primary focus of the visit must remain prayer and Communion. If a person is lonely, the parish may be able to offer other visitors at another time. The eucharistic minister has a different and specific commitment, particularly if we take Communion to more than one housebound person each week, though over time they may become personal friends. If this balance is problematical and you feel that a housebound person has unrealistic expectations, a quiet talk with the parish priest may help to resolve the difficulty.

This is also the first step to resolving other problems. Sick and housebound people are not always patient and gentle. They may be angry about their condition, drink too much or develop mental problems. Alternatively, they may be poorly housed, badly cared for or even ill treated. The parish community has a duty of pastoral care to its members, but this does not mean that individual eucharistic ministers must put up with abuse, nor should you feel obliged to give other kinds of assistance. Few lay people have professional training in this field and we should not feel guilty that we cannot do more. Larger parishes, with many ministers taking Communion to the sick, may wish to prepare guidelines for them or even set out a parish policy on getting involved. Preparatory meetings to explain the wider aspects of taking Communion to the housebound may also be useful. So too might be a mentoring system that gives access to professional advice and/or a more experienced minister.

Safeguarding the vulnerable

Ministers of Communion often visit vulnerable people. Recent legislation may require police checks to be done before they start work. Ideally, the person's family and friends should always be present when Communion is given, to share in the prayer and fellowship, but many housebound people live alone.

Those who receive Communion at home regularly should be visited by a priest at intervals anyway, but they (and a neighbour or friend also) ought to have a contact number to report any odd incidents or worries. We do not want to make them fearful or overly suspicious, but we do have a duty to protect the vulnerable, especially when the parish asks them to welcome and trust a eucharistic minister. Equally, we may need to protect eucharistic ministers from false accusations.

In usual parish circumstances, the priest will check with sick or housebound people (or their families) that they would like to be brought Communion and are willing for a lay person to do this. Ideally, we will accompany the priest on our first visit, but otherwise we should telephone them first. We should never visit unexpectedly, nor take other visitors with us unless this has been previously agreed. Often, we will settle into a routine of visiting at a fixed time once a week or so and then only need to call if the routine is changed. We need to have the telephone number of the person we visit, or a contact, and they need to have ours (they may need to change the appointment, too). Data Protection legislation means we must give permission for this exchange and we should not pass on other people's telephone numbers without their agreement.

Practical preparations for the visit

When we take Communion to someone at home or in hospital, we need a small table or other flat surface on which to place the pyx. We may find that every space around the sick person is covered with necessary items. In this case, we should ask carers to make room or ask permission to do it ourselves (remembering where things were, so as to put them back in the right places afterwards). In this space we place the corporal (square linen cloth) and set the pyx on it. As the traditional sign of the presence of the Blessed Sacrament a candle or tea-light may be lit, unless there are clinical or practical reasons not to do this.

The rite of Communion of the sick is published as a booklet by McCrimmons and is easy to follow. The parish should supply a copy of this, or a customized version, along with a pyx and linens to those who take Communion to the sick and housebound. An extra copy or copies of *Communion of the Sick* may help the sick person and others present to make the responses. (Although these are familiar from Mass, these people do not get to Mass very often and so the words may not be recalled easily.) A people's *Sunday Missal* is useful if Mass readings and prayers are to be shared. In fact, this would be an excellent gift to each housebound person from the parish. The rite of *viaticum* and prayers for the dying are in one or more separate books, which the parish will make available if needed. Housebound people often like to provide a cloth, water, candles, even flowers, and prepare a table for the eucharistic minister's visit. They may also want to use their own Bible or read something from a favourite prayerbook.

The shape of the rite

The rite of Communion of the sick can be fairly informal, though it should conform to a recognizable pattern. There should be a first greeting as the minister arrives, making clear that this is a Communion visit and not just a social call, but it may be necessary to make the sick person comfortable and gather the household before the more formal greeting of the rite is spoken.

Elements of the rite will be familiar from Mass: placing ourselves in God's presence, a penitential preparatory rite, sharing of scripture, the Lord's Prayer, the giving of Communion and concluding rites. However, there is considerable latitude within this structure. During the Easter season, the sprinkling of holy water might replace the 'I confess'. Hymns and intercessions can be included and silence or a meditation may follow the scripture reading(s).

When visiting during the week, it is customary to share one or more of the readings from the previous Sunday, unless the person visited prefers to choose and prepare some other biblical text. In many parishes, the minister brings a copy of the parish newsletter and suggests some item that needs prayer. Alternatively, the housebound person may be the prayer partner of someone in a sacramental preparation programme.

The pyx

Ministers carry the consecrated bread in a pyx. This may be given to them after Communion at Sunday Mass, so that they can go straight to the sick or housebound and keep fresh the link with the Sunday assembly of the faithful. At other times, ministers may be trusted to go to the tabernacle and fill the pyx themselves. Parish arrangements vary considerably. Some only have one or two shared pyxes, which must be returned to the church after each visit. Others provide a pyx for each minister who visits the sick regularly. (There should also be some arrangement to wash the corporals and purificators used on visits to the sick.)

A pyx is generally enclosed in a small cloth bag with long strings, so that it can be hung around the neck. However, any safe carrying place is acceptable – an inside coat pocket or a secure handbag. Very occasionally, someone who cannot take solid food will receive the precious blood instead. This is taken straight from Mass in a small, air-tight phial. Of course, ministers who are carrying the Blessed Sacrament should go directly to their destination. There is no reason to snub people we may meet on the way, but we should be brief and perhaps make arrangements to talk later.

On arrival, the minister opens out the corporal on the table, lays the pyx on it and opens the pyx before the rite begins. It is helpful to have water available, both to help a sick person swallow the host and so that the minister can clean the pyx once it is empty. The purificator is used for this and may be placed on the lap or beneath the chin of the one receiving Communion if spills are likely.

Sometimes the minister will have more visits to make and will simply close the pyx, put it back in a safe place and move on. Usually we would take only the number of hosts or fragments we know we will need, but, if there has been some miscalculation, we should consume any that remain. If Communion is to be given in form of wine, a drop may be placed on the tongue directly from the carrying phial or it may be poured into a small chalice or wine glass and sipped from there. We should consume anything that remains and carefully clean the vessels with water afterwards. Once we are no longer carrying the Blessed Sacrament, we can go off to other work or stay for tea and a chat.

The minister as messenger

While eucharistic ministers must respect confidences, we may also act as messengers, carrying information and requests back to the parish clergy and bringing news of parish events. If we visit more than one person in an afternoon (or are forgetful), we might like to carry a small notebook and pen to be sure that we pass on any messages correctly. Eucharistic ministers do not replace the pastoral ministry of the priest, but our frequent visits may enable us to mention a desire for the sacrament of reconciliation (confession), warn of a sick person's decline or, indeed, announce recovery and a joyful return to normal life.

All in all, taking Communion to the sick and housebound is very different from giving Communion in church. Yet, it is a hugely rewarding ministry for those who like meeting people and who have some free time. It is sometimes presented as suitable for active retired people, but ministers of any age are acceptable. Indeed, older housebound people often enjoy seeing a younger person and it is a great confidence booster to be entrusted with such a ministry. There is also great value in peer ministry – nothing should prevent, say, a wheelchair user who is otherwise fairly independent from taking Communion to the homes of housebound people, where there is suitable access.

Eucharistic ministers feel privileged to take Communion to people in their own homes or in hospital. They often report that those who receive Communion, far from demanding sympathy and attention for themselves, offer support and a warm welcome to the minister. So, often, we will find that we go out to minister to another and are showered with blessings ourselves.

Questions to ponder and discuss

How is the pastoral care of sick and housebound people currently provided in your parish or community? (You may need to ask your parish priest for an outline.) Do lay eucharistic ministers have a part in this? Could they do more?

Think about sick or housebound Catholics you have known. Would it have made a difference if you had been able to take them Communion regularly and assure them of the remembrance and prayers of the parish family?

Copies of the following checklists may be made for each person the minister visits. The list of things provided by the person visited does not indicate what they ought to provide – it is merely a memory aid for the eucharistic minister of what they like to provide and, thus, to some extent, of the way they prefer to celebrate.

The first four items on the minister's list are essential. The next few should be brought unless the communicant will provide them. The final few are optional.

Taking Communion to: [fill in name of individual or group]
At: [give address]
Tel:
Usual day and time of visit:

Communicant provides	✓
Clean table covering	
Glass of drinking water (for personal use)	
Water in a jug (for minister's use)	
Candles (and matches)	
Sunday (or weekday) Missal	
Bible	
Favourite prayerbook	
Flowers	
Other items [list]	

Minister brings	✓
Pyx containing consecrated bread (or phial of wine and chalice)	
Corporal	
Purificator	
Communion of the Sick booklet	
Small, leakproof bottle of water	
Missal or Bible	
Holy water	
Newsletter	
Other items [list]	

Usual form of Communion service		✓
Opening	Simple greeting only	
	Penitential rite (set form or variable?)	
	Vary by season (e.g. sprinkling of water)	
	Song/hymn	
Word	One short reading only	
	Two or more readings	
	Psalm	
	Silence/meditation	
	Sharing/discussion	
	Formal intercessions	
	Spontaneous prayer	
Communion	List practical requirements	
Conclusion	Thanksgiving prayer	
	Other prayers	
	Vary form of blessing	
	Song/hymn	
Communicant will prepare reading(s)		
Communicant will lead prayers		
Communicant will choose songs/hymns		
Other things to remember [list]		

8

'Let Nothing Disturb You'

We wouldn't be human if we didn't have some worries about doing something as important as giving the body and blood of Christ to others. This chapter discusses some of the most frequently voiced questions and comments. In general, though, the best people to talk to are your fellow eucharistic ministers. They will be able to calm your fears and remind you of parts of your training you may have forgotten.

I'm not worthy to give Communion

None of us is: 'All have sinned and lack God's glory', Paul told the Romans (3:23, NJB), before adding, 'and all are justified by the free gift of his grace'. In other words, all of us have been made worthy. We do not have to be any more worthy to give Communion than to receive it and we are all encouraged to receive Communion frequently. Faith is what counts, not age or status in the community or even a sense of worth.

I'm nervous

Everyone finds it tough to do something new in public. Distributing Communion is one of the easier things because you are giving people their heart's desire. They come to you with thanksgiving, not to criticize your technique. You will settle into it very quickly, but meanwhile there are a few simple calming exercises that may help.

- Make sure you stand comfortably, with your feet slightly apart and shoulders relaxed.
- Take a few slow, deep breaths.
- Loosen your grip on the Communion dish or chalice if you are holding them too tightly.
- Look at the person receiving Communion and focus on their meeting with the Lord, not on yourself.
- Say a quick prayer for confidence.
- Remember that no two ministers give Communion in exactly the same way. It's not wrong or a mistake to be different.

What if I drop the host or spill the wine?

Accidents happen, though we are so aware how precious the gifts are that we share at Communion that spills are very rare. The first rule to follow if it does happen, though, is not to panic. The second is to be reassured that we have not committed a grave sacrilege, nor, indeed, any sin at all.

If you drop a host or fragment of one, calmly bend down and pick it up. Either consume it yourself immediately or set it apart in the Communion dish and do so at the end of Communion. A communicant who drops the host ought to do likewise, but, if they freeze, you should do it for them. If you think you dropped a crumb too small to see, you do not need to do anything. A crumb cannot be broken and shared and so is not a sacramental sign.

If you should ever drop the chalice, pick it up and use your purificator to mop up as much liquid as possible. Put this in the chalice and use another to cover the spot until Mass ends. Make sure that the priest knows what happened and he will do the rest.

We are much more likely to spill tiny drops of the consecrated wine on the altar cloth or our own clothes than anything else. These drops should be rinsed with cold water after Mass and can then be laundered as usual. Again, as we cannot take and drink these spots of wine, there is no sacramental significance.

If you've had an accident, simply deal with it and forget about it. Don't go on worrying about it. Don't reproach yourself or allow other people to do so. Don't lose confidence in yourself as a minister.

How do I know if a child is old enough to receive Communion?

If in doubt, look at the parent for reassurance. Otherwise, read the signs – children who hold their hands out confidently and with respect have surely been prepared for Communion, while those who are looking sideways to copy older siblings are probably too young.

In the long term, we will probably come to recognize the children of our own community who are preparing for first Communion as then we can welcome them appropriately.

Can I receive Communion twice in one day?

Yes, at distinct celebrations. If you are eucharistic minister at more than one Mass in a day, you should be seen to receive Communion yourself at each. Also, if you celebrate a Communion service with a housebound person some time after a Mass, you may, if you wish to, receive again with them (but not if you make brief visits to several people in hospital). However, if you take someone Communion direct from Sunday Mass without some time elapsing, you should choose whether to receive Communion with them or with the parish community as this is effectively a single celebration.

The rite of Communion is a single entity, so eucharistic ministers who receive at the start and then consume any remaining bread or wine at the end are not receiving Communion a second time.

Why can't we use small hosts?

It is not forbidden and many communities still do, but the larger host is a better sign of our communion in Christ as it must be broken into many parts before it is shared. The Breaking of Bread is one of the ancient names for the Eucharist. The liturgy assumes that this will take some time and provides a litany to be sung during it ('Lamb of God').

In the same way, it would be better if we all shared one cup, but this is not practical for a large number of people. Many communities keep the wine in one large flagon, or a pouring chalice (an oversized, lipped chalice) during the eucharistic prayer, and then transfer it to smaller chalices just before Communion. This way, it is easier to see that we all share the one cup than if a row of chalices had been on the altar throughout.

I've caught a cold

Use your common sense. If you can't stop coughing and sneezing or fear the illness is contagious, ask a fellow minister to take your place.

Wine is mildly antiseptic, so there is little risk of catching minor ailments from a shared chalice. However, those who are infectious (and those who cannot easily fight off infections) sometimes prefer to receive Communion by intinction, that is, dipping the host partway into the chalice.

Can I give Communion in the parish school, in a local residential home or a prison?

Yes, if you are asked to do so, have the necessary training and are commissioned for these places. If you are a parish eucharistic minister, you can serve anywhere within the parish, but it is helpful to be recommissioned or otherwise introduced to groups who might not recognize you.

When you go to serve another community, make sure to learn their customs and expectations. If possible, watch their present minister at work before you take over.

We had a visiting priest who did things differently

Visitors can cause confusion, either because they have a different style of presiding or because they don't know your community's customs. In an ideal world, priest and people would be of one mind liturgically. In practice, lay ministers need to be extra alert when there is a supply priest and not get flustered. We should do our usual work confidently, but be adaptable to any changes.

Should we give Communion under both kinds at school Masses?

When children are old enough to receive Communion, they are old enough to receive under both kinds. We may prefer to use wine with a lower alcohol content (though it must still be pure wine) or the priest may be generous when he adds a 'drop' of water. If the local education authority forbids alcohol on school premises, you need to obtain a dispensation for altar wine. At school Masses, like any other, we need to emphasize the 'greater sign'.

However, this raises wider questions. First, are there more suitable forms of liturgy for a class of infants? It would be considered rude if we invited friends for a meal then told them they could not have anything themselves, only watch us eat. Yet this is how the Mass must seem to young children. Second, are compulsory school Masses appropriate for young people who do not otherwise choose to participate in liturgy? The invitation to Communion implies a real relationship with Christ and his Church and a desire to nourish and strengthen it.

Can I bless a person who is not receiving Communion?

We can all pray blessings on others at any time. However, in our role as a eucharistic minister, it is more appropriate to say something simple like 'God bless you', perhaps with a light touch on the shoulder. The more formal 'May almighty God bless you . . .' should be used by a priest.

Should lay eucharistic ministers be part of the entry procession and sit in the sanctuary throughout Mass?

Not routinely. It is a much better witness to be seen in the midst of the community, taking a full part in the liturgy and approaching the altar only when needed. We try not to seem set apart from other lay people, nor to identify with the ordained ministers.

What should we wear?

Clothes should be comfortable, practical and non-controversial. Parishes sometimes offer guidelines on jeans, fashion wear and summer casuals – these will be more acceptable if most parishioners wear similar clothes to Mass. Otherwise, choose neutral colours and styles as we should be neither the focus of attention nor a distraction. Shoes need to have non-slip soles and shouldn't be noisy when we walk. Wide sleeves, trailing scarves and fussy trimmings can be nuisances. Unless it is very cold, take off coats or other outerwear before coming to the altar (otherwise we may look as if we are in a hurry to leave). Come empty-handed to the altar, leaving any bags, missals and so on with a friend.

Lay eucharistic ministers should not wear clerical dress. The only vestment that is rightfully ours is the alb – the white garment of all the baptized – but it is not customary to wear it in the UK.

In most parishes, the eucharistic ministers will be well enough known not to need special identification. In very big communities or at special events a badge or lapel-pin is probably sufficient – sashes make us look like ushers. Lay ministers should not wear stoles.

Should I smile and use people's names when I give them Communion?

In the UK, traditionally we have been advised against using people's names at Communion, either because it is not the custom to use names frequently in conversation or to avoid causing offence to those whose names we do not know. However, as people are addressed by name at baptism, confirmation and other sacraments, there seems no reason to avoid it absolutely at Communion.

A gentle, welcoming, facial expression seems very appropriate at Communion, but not a conspiratorial grin.

Somebody came up for Communion who is not a Catholic

Non-Catholics who come for a blessing at Communion should indicate this by crossing their arms on their chests. A few forget or assume we recognize them.

Communion is not the time to get into a theological discussion, so generally Communion should be given to everyone who follows Catholic customs and comes reverently to receive with every sign of faith.

If you know that someone who received Communion is not Catholic, tell the priest after Mass.

I'm a reader and a eucharistic minister

You must feel greatly blessed. Normally you will only exercise one of these ministries in any given celebration, so that others can serve the community, too. Your flexibility will be very useful, though, especially at holiday times.

Make sure that the people who draw up the rotas for readers and eucharistic ministers communicate with each other so that you are not listed for both ministries at the same Mass. If you are, you will have to choose which to do, and ask the rota-makers to find someone else to do the other. (This is better than finding your own replacement, because it will make them mindful of the problem in future.)

It is natural to be slightly nervous about being a eucharistic minister, for we are entrusted with the mysteries of God.

With common sense, respect and a responsible attitude, we will deal confidently with any problems that arise.

We can turn to fellow ministers for encouragement and advice.

Questions to ponder and discuss

What kind of person am I? Confident, happy-go-lucky, quiet, a worrier . . . ?

How can I use my personality to good advantage in the eucharistic ministers' group?

What is my greatest worry or fear about giving Communion?

Why does this, in particular, bother me so much? What might I do to ease my fears?

9

A Continuing Ministry

Becoming a eucharistic minister is not a long or difficult process if we have faith and goodwill. However, part of our commitment is to make sure we carry on being good eucharistic ministers.

When we nervously come up to minister for the first time, it seems impossible that we would ever take such a privilege for granted. After a time, though, when the routine is familiar, it is all too easy to go through it without thinking overly much about what we are doing. We settle down with our fellow ministers, too, and can get a bit too comfortable about expecting them to cover our absences. This is part of the reason why our bishops want ministers to attend a day of study and recollection each year. It is our annual check-up, when we are reminded to protect and nourish our ministry and our whole Christian life. Of course, our spiritual health must be tended daily.

Mostly, what makes us better eucharistic ministers is what makes us better Christians. We all need to feed our Christian life each day. We choose to make time for personal prayer and the prayerful reading of scripture, despite being busy. We are full and active participants in Sunday Mass and sometimes in weekday Mass, too, or group devotions. We need to go on learning in the way that suits us – perhaps a course at deanery or diocesan level, a parish group, a challenging book or simply thinking through, in an adult way, material we are sharing with children in a Communion preparation programme, for example. We build our community by sharing in parish activities, work activities, neighbourhood activities. Above all, we remember that everyday life is holy, too – the sacred can be found in the most mundane of deeds.

Prayer, the first essential

Prayer is important. 'Pray as you can, not as you can't' (Abbot John Chapman) is excellent advice. We can aspire to the heights of contemplative prayer, but in reality many of our prayers during the day are of the 'Please, God' or 'Help!' kind – and rightly so. We should be able to talk with God about people we meet and things that happen, even the most mundane. Sometimes we even remember to say thanks. Another of Chapman's aphorisms is that the less we pray the worse it gets. The quality of our prayer may dissatisfy us, but the simple act of turning to God is pleasing to him. God does not need our prayers, but he seems to delight in them, as parents enjoy their children's company. Often we need to listen more and worry less about the ways in which we pray.

At the same time, we will never discover the many ways in which we *can* pray unless we are willing to experiment. Praying with others is a good way to pick up ideas, as well as adding an extra dimension to our praying. When we sing, we pray twice, said Augustine, while Dominic prayed through movement when he was too weary for words. For time set aside specifically for prayer, many of us prefer some kind of structure, whether it be a version of the Office, the rosary or the morning and evening prayers we were taught as children. It can be helpful to use other people's words when ours seem inadequate. Sometimes, though, we just need to sit in silence, realizing that all words are inadequate before the face of God.

Nurturing our ministry

Once we have settled into ministry, we can concentrate on the wider aspects of it. We can look with God's love on the people coming to receive Communion, welcome them in our hearts and pray for them. We can find ways to be supportive of fellow ministers, especially those in training, and the parish clergy. We might leave more time to calm and prepare ourselves before Mass. We should certainly allow ourselves to wonder at the mystery that is opened up to us at every Mass and give thanks that we are part of it in such an intimate way.

One way in which we can specifically nurture our ministry is to share fellowship and build up friendships with fellow ministers, for mutual help and encouragement. Curiously, liturgical ministers often forget to pray together or else limit it to quick opening and closing prayers surrounding other things. Social events (or a social conclusion to a working meeting) are not optional or a waste of time. As we work as a team, it is useful to get to know the strengths of others and discover any difficulties that affect their ministry. Somehow, it is easier to be responsible and reliable when we see what problems are caused otherwise. It is certainly better to understand a fellow minister's troubles than let resentments build up.

Resolving resentments

In general, liturgical ministers tend to be a peaceable group, but it is good practice to deal with any problems quickly and not let them fester. In some parishes a buddy system is helpful. With this system, ministers work in pairs to offer each other encouragement, reminders and gentle criticism, if needed.

Ministers can get annoyed when others are unreliable and they have to fill in at the last moment. It is always stressful when something goes wrong. Of course, accidents and the unexpected happen, but we can still find it upsetting. Squabbles, jealousy and blaming others are common human failings and we certainly do not want to give them room to grow within the ministers' group. Very, very rarely, two ministers come into open conflict and then neither of them should minister until they are reconciled. As eucharistic ministers, we ought to be examples of tolerance, forgiveness and unselfishness for fellow parishioners.

(Almost) trouble-free rotas

Probably the biggest cause of annoyance is the rota. There is no one, simple, foolproof way to decide who will minister when. It is for your group to find a method that suits you well enough and causes fewest upsets.

In some parishes, every minister's availability is checked before the rota is drawn up. This may mean that some names appear more frequently than others. It need not be a problem, unless some ministers feel overlooked and others overworked. Other parishes just cycle ministers' names in alphabetical order and leave them to arrange their own swaps if necessary. Still others assign ministers to a specific Sunday of each month. Pity the poor folk who draw the fifth Sunday!

A sign-up system is an alternative to a drawn-up rota, but it may mean that the same few people always fill the best slots while nobody wants the less popular times. Sign-ups work best as a preliminary to making a rota for holiday seasons, when people may be away. Ministers can indicate all the services they plan to attend, but will only be asked to give Communion at some of them.

Experience recommends that one person be in overall charge of the rota, or at least one person for each Mass-time, and it should, ideally, be a long-term commitment. If this person is a eucharistic minister, so much the better. He or she is more likely to watch, listen and make adjustments, so that, for example, the less reliable people are not all listed together. Ministers should have some input, but the rota-maker needs to draw up the final scheme and the rota should not then be changed without his or her agreement. Making a rota is a thankless task; it is rare that everyone is totally satisfied. It goes without saying that rude or aggressive responses should not be tolerated.

Computers have taken away the practical difficulties of making out a rota, though some folk still prefer to move around slips of paper with names on first. Remember to liaise with the readers' rota-maker if people exercise both ministries, so that they are not listed to do both at the same Mass. If you are storing ministers' addresses, telephone numbers and other personal details on a computer, you must conform with data protection legislation.

Keep reviewing the work

Although a study and retreat day each year is essential, it may be useful for eucharistic ministers to meet more often, even as frequently as once a month. Often our initial training just covers the basics. It can be helpful to go over the practical aspects of our work periodically and also take time to explore the eucharistic liturgy or some of the themes in this book more fully.

Ministers do best when they are sure of what is expected of them. Parish clergy and eucharistic ministers should try to agree a basic routine (which can then be adapted to suit specific Masses). It is not helpful if each presider has different expectations and practices. It may be useful to have written guidelines and update them when the routine is changed. Lay ministers are not the priest's helpers so much as the community's servants. Priests and lay ministers work together, so each should *know* what the other will do, not have to guess it. There must be mutual respect.

Personal prayer, pondering scripture, active participation in Sunday Mass, learning more about our faith, sharing in parish activities, discovering the sacred in everyday life – these are some of the ways in which we grow as Christians.

Regular meetings for friendship and fellowship with other lay eucharistic ministers nurture our ministry.

Questions to ponder and discuss

Whether you are a new or experienced eucharistic minister, how do you feel about your ministry? Do you think your attitudes have changed/will change with time?

What do you most need to go on being a good minister? (A babysitter, a spiritual director, more hours in the day – think widely!) Can you organize it?

End this session with a fairly long time of prayer. If you wish, read 1 Corinthians 10:16–17 or another suitable scripture passage. Make sure that you keep silence for a time, as well as praying familiar prayers or spontaneously. Sing if you like! Conclude with the opening prayer of last Sunday's Mass (from a Sunday Missal) or another of your choice.

10

A Minister Forever?

We became servants of God and of our fellow human beings at baptism and cannot cease to be so. However, the ways in which we serve change with age and circumstances. It would be inappropriate for a young child to be a minister of Communion – children first learn to serve in small ways and grow in ability and responsibility. In adult life, opportunities for service in the wider community may be few while we are working long hours and bringing up a family, though liturgical ministry may fit into the scheme quite well. After all, we would come to Sunday Mass with the family, anyway. Eventually, age and infirmity may limit the ways in which we can give of ourselves and we will need the grace to let others serve us.

When to stop?

Being a eucharistic minister is not a life sentence. If there is a crisis or life is just starting to get too busy, we can, at any time, ask to be removed from the rota for a while or permanently. Nor is giving Communion our only option. Some people decide that five or ten years is enough and then transfer to some other ministry. If being a eucharistic minister becomes boring or frustrating or simply part of our routine, it's probably time to move on.

It is much more difficult when the parish community has to ask someone to stop giving Communion. There can be many reasons. A person may have such a disordered life that, though they want to minister, they just cannot bear the responsibility. Many parishes have a long-serving lay minister who grows so slowly into ill health or mental confusion that there is no obvious moment to retire. Who is willing to say something? Occasionally a minister is convicted of a crime or discovered in some moral failing that causes scandal in the community and forfeits our confidence in them. As a community of forgiveness, we may eventually have to ask ourselves if we will welcome back to ministry somebody who has served their time and repented.

The annual recommissioning

Lay eucharistic ministers are recommissioned annually, often on the Sunday after the annual study and recollection day. This is a good moment to ask ourselves if we are content to continue or if it is time to move to another ministry. There should be no shame in this and no coercion to stay on from fellow ministers. Of course, we will try to give sufficient notice so new ministers can be trained to replace us. It is probably healthy for a parish to see new faces among its team of eucharistic ministers and to recognize former eucharistic ministers now serving the community in other ways. It reminds everyone that all are called to serve – a parish is not divided into liturgical ministers and others. Theoretically, everyone who receives Communion is a past, present or future eucharistic minister.

Lay ministers are commissioned for their own parish or a specific community in which they will work. If we move home and become part of a new parish community, we have no automatic right to be a eucharistic minister there. However, it is always worthwhile mentioning our previous ministry when we make ourselves known to the new parish priest. Some people even take a letter, a kind of reference, from their old parish with them. There are parishes that will need our skills badly and recommission us immediately. Others will prefer that we settle in and learn their customs first. If acceptance seems slow, all we can do is be patient and gentle with our reminders.

A positive move

A person who decides to stop being a eucharistic minister is not a fail-
ure, nor should they feel that they are putting the remaining ministers
under extra pressure. Almost invariably, that person will have given
loyal service to the parish community, often for very many years, and
deserves our thanks. It is probably unwise to continue to minister
when our heart is no longer in it. There is a certain pride in thinking
that we are indispensable. However, it is better by far to help train
our successors and then move on gracefully to some different form of
service than go through the motions or put undue stress on ourselves.

Even then, we may reconsider our decision in years to come. Frequent changes of mind are not good for the parish in general or the
ministers' group in particular, but it should be possible for a trained
minister to return to the work after a break. It is even possible, with
goodwill, to accommodate eucharistic ministers who live abroad for
part of the year or who are away at college during term-time.

Above all, we should be glad when we can serve our parish as
eucharistic ministers, but not feel guilty when we are no longer able
to or feel called to some other ministry. We are not reneging on our
baptismal commitment or ceasing to be servants in Christ's image.
As Paul reminds us, 'There are many different ways of serving, but
it is always the same Lord' (1 Corinthians 12:5, NJB). We have been
greatly privileged to give the bread of life and the cup of salvation
to others. Now it will be our delight to discover what new ways of
serving the Lord has in mind for us.

We are called to serve God and our neighbour throughout our
lives, but we will have different ministries at different times.

We cease to be eucharistic ministers when we can no longer
do the work or no longer wish to.

With gratitude for the privilege we have enjoyed of sharing
Christ with others, we look for new ways to serve.

Questions to ponder and discuss

When should a lay eucharistic minister 'retire'?

How do we receive lay liturgical ministers moving into our parish? Is it better to involve them quickly or should they have a year to get to know our traditions first?

11

Services in the Absence of a Priest

Communion of the sick is not the only liturgy at which a lay minister can preside. In many parts of the world, isolated Catholic communities think Mass every Sunday is an unattainable luxury. They may see a priest once a month or less frequently and so their daily liturgy is led by a lay presider. The Church has acknowledged this reality in the document *Directory on Sunday Celebrations in the Absence of a Priest* (1988), which recommends that the people gather every Sunday for a liturgy of the word (or morning or evening prayer) and Communion.

In the UK, we can still generally find Sunday Mass within reasonable distance of home, but weekday Masses may be cancelled, especially at holiday times. In 1998, the Bishops' Conference of England and Wales published *One Bread, One Body* as a reflection on the whole issue. One outcome has been the development of Services of Word and Communion, which are likely to become more familiar to us in years to come.

Sunday: the faithful gather

There are two distinct considerations here. The first is the unique nature of Sunday as *the* day to celebrate the Eucharist. We have seen that Sunday was the only day for the Eucharist in the early Church, and it remains the only day of the week on which we are obliged to attend Mass. Sunday Mass forms and builds up the Church as no other celebration can. For this reason, the main emphasis is on making every effort to gather the faithful for Mass on Sunday, even if they have to meet at a different time, travel to another parish or congregate in larger numbers than usual. If even one Mass is celebrated on Sunday (or Saturday evening) in a locality, it is not permitted also to have a Sunday Celebration in the Absence of a Priest. In England and Wales, we may have to change our attitudes somewhat if Sunday Mass no longer fits conveniently into our routine, but we can rarely claim that Mass is unavailable.

The very act of coming to Mass on Sunday is a proclamation of our faith and commitment and a witness to the world.

One Bread, One Body, 54

Taking part in the Mass is the hallmark of the Catholic, central and crucial to our Catholic identity.

One Bread, One Body, 3

Weekday Mass, on the other hand, gives more emphasis to personal (though not private) devotion and less to the ecclesial nature of worship. On Sundays, the whole Church gathers; on weekdays, a smaller gathering represents the whole body of the Church. However, as priests grow fewer and older and take on more duties, they are not always available to celebrate Mass on weekdays.

A Service of Word and Communion is a way for lay people to satisfy their desire for daily Communion, especially if this has been their habit for many years. It is also a means by which they can gather to pray for their community and a powerful symbol within that community of continuing unity from Sunday to Sunday. However, in some dioceses, there is a fear of abuse or creeping clericalism among the laity and so only a liturgy of the word (without Communion) is permitted.

> The Mass, like the whole of our Christian faith and discipleship, should be something deeply personal, but never private.
>
> *One Bread, One Body, 56*

The daily and weekly cycles of prayer

As priests become fewer and busier, lay people can also maintain their community's weekly schedule of prayer and devotions, including worship of the Eucharist outside of Mass. They may expose the Blessed Sacrament for public veneration and lead Benediction (with minor changes to the rite). Already, the Prayer of the Church (the full daily Office or just morning and evening prayer) is frequently led by lay people. Of course, popular devotions and group prayer have long been shared by groups of Catholics, with no special authority or mandate, in church or in their homes, with or without an ordained minister. The Church has a duty to foster faith and meet the needs of the faithful, so far as is practicable. This is not the priest's duty alone, though, and it seems probable that we will see lay people leading non-sacramental liturgy ever more frequently.

> The celebration of the Eucharist, as also of the entire liturgy, is carried out by means of signs perceptible to the senses – signs by means of which faith is nourished, strengthened and expressed. Hence all possible care should be taken that, from the rites and ceremonies proposed by the Church, those should be chosen which, in view of individual and local circumstances, will best foster active participation and meet the needs of the faithful.
>
> *General Instruction on the Roman Missal, 1970, 1/5*

The art of presiding

It is important to understand that presiding at liturgy is a separate and different ministry and so different skills are needed. At present, though, we tend to ask a lay eucharistic minister or reader to take on the role when we celebrate a Service of Word and Communion as we do it infrequently. Eucharistic ministers are also sometimes asked to lead Benediction or exposition of the Blessed Sacrament, presumably because they will handle the Blessed Sacrament with confidence and respect. The art of presiding is a book in itself, so this chapter can only give a general outline of this ministry for those who are new to it.

Services of Word and Communion in the absence of a priest – whether the main Sunday celebration or smaller community gatherings during the week – need a presider, reader and eucharistic minister(s) as a minimum. On Sundays, all the usual liturgical ministers should be involved: servers, musicians, cantor and others. Normally, it is preferable for lay people to exercise only one ministry in any given liturgy, but, just as the priest-presider is also a minister of Communion, the lay presider may do likewise.

Feeding on the word

In normal circumstances, ministers are never permitted simply to distribute Communion. The Church always requires some sharing of the word first, with prayer and thanksgiving. The liturgy is to be ceremonious and celebratory, even though it is simpler than Mass. Indeed, Services of Word and Communion seem very like Mass unless we pay full attention (and this is why they cause some worry).

There are preparatory rites, a liturgy of the word, intercessions (and possibly even a homily on Sunday). The one thing that is always omitted is the consecratory eucharistic prayer. Thus, no gifts of bread and wine are brought to the altar. Sometimes a very simple prayer of thanksgiving is offered instead. Otherwise, after silence, and song if we wish, we move straight to the Our Father and the Communion rite.

The gifting and gifted communities

Christ has given the power to transform bread and wine into his body and blood to priests and bishops alone. In the Catholic tradition, only a male ordained to this ministry can offer the eucharistic prayer on our behalf – not even a deacon can do it. We are able to have a Communion service because, at an earlier time, priest and people celebrated the Eucharist together. Mindful of us and our needs, they shared their sacred meal with us, leaving pre-consecrated hosts for us. At their gathering, they surely prayed for us and, in like manner, we ought to give thanks for the eucharistic community that provided for us. If the tabernacle had been left empty, there could be no Communion rite. We would feast only on the word of God at our gathering. Of course, some of us may have been present at that earlier gathering, too, thus building a further link between these two groups who assemble for worship, a further reminder that we are one body in Christ.

The role of the presider

The role of the presider, whether lay or ordained, is to lead the community in prayer and to empower other ministers and the people to take full part in the liturgy. The presider's authority is that of the loyal and trusted servant who runs the household, not one who lords it over others. Good presiders do not try to do everything themselves, nor do they feel they must direct other ministers in their usual tasks. On a practical level, though, if a community celebrates a Service of Word and Communion only occasionally, it is helpful for the lay presider to check quietly that the preparations have been thought through. For example, the tabernacle key will be needed, but bread and wine should not be set out.

A lay presider must be accepted by the community he or she serves – how else could they represent and pray in the name of that community before God? The ministry may need to be introduced gently by the parish clergy as both necessary and valuable. New lay presiders gain confidence as they grow into the ministry. Unless we are used to leading meetings in our professional lives, we may be quite scared at first and feel foolish, just when we most want to seem calm and in control. Prayer will help us come to know that we are doing God's work and he will support us. Being human, though, we will also need to feel warmth and support from the people of our community.

Someone who takes on the ministry of lay presider regularly will learn many new skills: speaking without strain in a large space, addressing people who choose to spread themselves widely, calling them to pray as one body. We will discover how to sit without slumping, stand gracefully, make liturgical gestures without seeming embarrassed, and time greetings and responses, as well as the rhythms of prayers spoken aloud.

We will also want to know something about the different forms of liturgical prayer so that we can grasp the general shape of various rites and be freed from unthinking dependence on a service book. It is useful to be able to find our way around ritual books such as the Roman Missal and lectionary. For this we need to know something about the organization of the liturgical year, its feasts and seasons.

Above all, we need to care about those we serve, so as to help them grow in prayer and love of God, which means, once again, tending our own spiritual lives and being humble before God.

Three signs and sources of unity – shared faith, shared Eucharist and shared ministry – belong together.

One Bread, One Body, 59

Getting started

This all sounds quite fearsome, but eucharistic ministers who only occasionally lead a Service of Word and Communion should not worry too much. The liturgical texts are very clear and, after a little practice and with the help of our fellow ministers, we should be able to speak and act with confidence. The books not only give texts to be read aloud but also rubrics, or instructions on what to do. Often there are options to choose from, so we need to read through the liturgy carefully beforehand and even mark in pencil the sections we plan to use. The watchful eye of a friend may prevent simple failings such as forgetting to omit alleluia in Lent or confusing weeks of the year with those of a season.

Generally, the readings of the Mass of the day are used and the reader should be able to find these in the lectionary and proclaim them at the proper time (including the Gospel, as no ordained minister is available). Prayers may be from the Mass of the day or other suitable prayers may be chosen. We may be fortunate and have a cantor for the psalm who will also encourage other singing. (Remember that there will be no eucharistic acclamations as there is no eucharistic prayer, but some other songs or acclamations may be included.) Somebody who presides regularly at the liturgy should expect to be involved in its planning and preparation, too. If we preside only occasionally, though, this work will have been done for us, no doubt.

The practical details

As the ministry of lay presider has so recently been revived, the practical details are still to be formalized. In theory, the appropriate vestment is an alb alone – the white robe of all the baptized – no stole or other liturgical garment. This would be appropriate for a large Sunday celebration, but a eucharistic minister who occasionally leads a weekday service and finds only ill-fitting or grubby garments in the sacristy cupboard may feel more comfortable presiding in their own clothes. Indeed, some dioceses insist on this, fearing that any kind of liturgical dress will confuse the faithful (though nobody thinks that altar servers' robes confer clerical status and these are also white baptismal garments).

In general, a lay presider should use the presider's chair, which is a symbol of the ministry and of service rather than status. It also tends to be placed in the best possible place to lead the liturgy, so, if we choose to sit somewhere else, we are handicapping ourselves unnecessarily. Here again, some dioceses require lay presiders to leave the chair empty and either to set a simpler seat beside it for their own use or even to preside from outside the sanctuary. It can appear that the fear of abuse outweighs the people's right to good liturgy.

No rite for commissioning a lay presider is included in liturgical books yet, though it would seem most necessary to present such a minister to the community, receive their approval and authorize the new minister to preside at services. The *Book of Blessings* contains commissioning rites for other liturgical ministers, which might act as a model for commissioning a lay presider, while the Liturgy Office of the Bishops' Conference of England and Wales continues to work on this. Meanwhile, a lay eucharistic minister who occasionally presides at a weekday Service of Word and Communion, at the invitation of the parish priest and with the warm acceptance of the faithful, should take this as mandate enough.

Lay people may lead most non-sacramental forms of the liturgy when a priest is not available, as well as devotions and group prayer.

It is very important that all the faithful gather for worship on Sundays.

New Services of Word and Communion in the Absence of a Priest are being developed so that the people may be nourished by the word of God and the Eucharist both on Sundays and weekdays.

Questions to ponder and discuss

Do I understand the difference between a Service of Word and Communion and Mass?

Why can a lay person preside at one but not the other?

How do I feel about a lay person leading a Service of Word and Communion in my own parish? How would I feel about doing it myself?

If there was a grave shortage of priests, how far would I be willing to travel for Sunday Mass? Would I be willing to change the pattern of my Sundays substantially to accommodate Mass at an inconvenient time?

12

Your Commitment

Day of study and recollection

Lay eucharistic ministers are required to attend a day of recollection every year. Normally the meeting includes a talk and discussion on a eucharistic theme, some input on ministry, theoretical or practical, and an opportunity for spiritual renewal and prayer. In many communities, ministers are recommissioned for the coming year at the close of the day, though, pastorally, it may be better to do this at Sunday Mass in front of the people the ministers will serve.

It is better for eucharistic ministers to have their own dedicated day, but in smaller communities it may be more convenient for all the liturgical ministers to share a study day or even for the meeting to be open to all who wish to attend. The theme of such a day will necessarily be more general (an overview of the Mass, perhaps), but forms a good basis for more specific teaching at shorter sessions through the year.

Inevitably, one or two ministers will miss the day for a good reason. They may be invited to sit down with a few fellow ministers later to go over the main points of the day. However, if many ministers are unable to attend, the meeting will need to rescheduled for a different day or time of day. Some imaginative thinking may even be required to come up with other ways in which to fulfil the requirement.

What, where, when?

There is no need to schedule basic practical training or retraining during the study day, unless a major change is to be made to the routine followed by all eucharistic ministers. Otherwise, short sessions at some other time, in the place we normally minister and tailored to specific needs, are preferable.

Where the meeting is held will depend very much on the community we are. Some groups want to get well away from their usual surroundings and have the resources to book a retreat house or conference centre for the day. Other groups would like to step aside from the bustle of daily life, but can spend only a modest sum. They may find a local convent willing to lend a room or two. Many successful days of recollection have been held in parish rooms, though participants have to be a little more disciplined and not slip off to do other tasks at quiet moments.

The format of the day will also depend, to some extent, on the community, though it should aim to achieve a balance between teaching, spiritual refreshment, prayer and community-building. The traditional start and end times (about 10am to 4pm) may not suit your group. Perhaps afternoon/evening would be better or a longer day but with a long lunch break. Remember, though, that your plans may be affected by the venue you pick and your speaker, if you choose to invite one.

The pattern of the day

In practical terms, we find it hard to concentrate on one thing for very long, so talks should not be much longer than 30 minutes, followed by comments and questions. Indeed, it may be better to split a talk into two or three linked sections, with time for responses after each. Two hour-long sessions like this are sufficient for an average parish group. The rest of the day will easily be filled with times of prayer and quiet, refreshment breaks and, perhaps, a general question and answer session or an open discussion on a topic of specific interest to the group. Mostly, it is hard to avoid trying to do too much while we are all together.

Having a guest speaker is useful in several respects. First, he or she will come with a new approach to the topic of your day, a new way of expressing eternal truths. This in itself is a refreshing change and it allows the community members who would otherwise lead the day to sit down and enjoy it. The mere fact that we are paying somebody to speak is a great aid to concentration. Guest speakers also have a way of raising topics that we in the community find hard to tackle among ourselves and a new pair of eyes spots problems we have chosen to ignore. Visiting speakers should be able to discuss any difficulties impartially, not being personally involved, leaving decisions to us. (They may even unite our group by acting as a focus for our annoyance!) Occasionally, a guest speaker acts as a go-between, helping us find common ground in our differing visions of ministry. If nothing else, we are more courteous when a stranger is present.

Prayer and refreshment

The form of prayer we choose will also depend on the group that gathers. A more traditional group may want Mass during the day, though we should not be celebrating apart from the community we serve on a Sunday (or late Saturday afternoon). Little and often is a good alternative prayer pattern: simple forms of morning, noon and evening prayer take only 10 to 15 minutes each and frame the day. If our study day happens to focus on eucharistic devotion, then we may want exposition and Benediction of the Blessed Sacrament instead. It is helpful to have a chapel or quiet prayer room available throughout the day. Whatever is decided on, it is best not to offer too many choices. Sacramental reconciliation, for example, is inappropriate unless it ties in strongly with the theme of the day.

Spiritual refreshment is difficult to engineer because it means different things to different people. For a busy mother, simply getting away for the day may be enough. Others will want time to themselves or a country walk, while those who are often alone may feel renewed by talking seriously with others. The great temptation when planning a study meeting like this is to fill every moment, forgetting that gaps in the schedule are often the most fruitful moments of the day. We do not need constantly to be busy to make the most of our time together. However, we may need to offer some guidance if the group simply mills around, waiting for the next item on the schedule to begin. Undemanding activities, such as kicking a ball about, may not seem at all spiritual, but they release any tension and make us more open to the work of God within us.

Nothing is wasted on a day of recollection. Even a seeming disaster, such as the heating breaking down in midwinter, creates a sense of solidarity. We might prefer the group to have a serious discussion on a eucharistic theme, but chatting and the sharing of experiences also build up the community. Coffee, lunch and tea breaks are useful pauses for strengthening friendships and consolidating the work of more formal sessions. Rather than suggesting people bring a packed lunch, ask them to bring food to share. It not only makes for a more interesting meal, it also echoes the Eucharist we share.

The annual day of recollection is most effectual when it is part of a year-round programme of prayer, learning, practical training and social events. This need not be burdensome. Brief, informal gatherings of small groups after Mass for some specific purpose can be as useful as a regular monthly meeting. However, the annual gathering should not seem to be separate or stand alone. Rather, it should be a time to consider and consolidate our ministry and the source of strength and inspiration for our continuing work.

Rite of commissioning lay eucharistic ministers

Lay eucharistic ministers are authorized and commissioned by the local bishop, though almost always the work is delegated to his representative (usually the parish priest or the chaplain of an institution). Ministers are normally commissioned for one year at a time, renewable annually. The commissioning includes taking Communion to the sick and dying, so that even if ministers are not yet trained for this, they may undertake the work later.

The rite most often takes place during Mass, immediately after the homily (in which it is recommended that some explanation of the ministry be given). If it takes place outside Mass, a short liturgy of the word is first celebrated.

Lay eucharistic ministers may be commissioned (and recommissioned) at any time convenient to the community they will serve. Corpus Christi is favoured by many. The Mass of the Lord's Supper on Maundy Thursday would also be suitable. However, the following rite is too long and would unbalance that service, so it would be simplified for that occasion. The rite is reproduced from the ritual texts of the International Commission on English in the Liturgy, for use in the United States, but it may be used for study purposes elsewhere.

Rite of Commissioning Special Ministers of Holy Communion

1. Persons authorized to distribute holy communion in special circumstances should be commissioned by the local Ordinary or his delegate[1] according to the following rite. The rite should take place in the presence of the people during Mass or outside Mass.

A. *During Mass*

2. In the homily the celebrant first explains the reason for his ministry and then presents to the people those chosen to serve as special ministers, using these or similar words:

Dear friends in Christ,
Our brothers and sisters N.* and N. are to be entrusted with administering the eucharist, with taking communion to the sick, and with giving it as viaticum to the dying.

The celebrant pauses, and then addresses the new ministers:

In this ministry, you must be examples of Christian living in faith and conduct; you must strive to grow in holiness through this sacrament of unity and love. Remember that, though many, we are one body because we share the one bread and one cup.
As ministers of holy communion be, therefore, especially observant

of the Lord's command to love your neighbour. For when he gave his body as food to his disciples, he said to them: 'This is my commandment, that you should love one another as I have loved you.'

3. After the address the candidates stand before the celebrant, who asks them these questions:

Are you resolved to undertake the office of giving the body and blood of the Lord to your brothers and sisters, and so serve to build up the Church?
R. I am.

Are you resolved to administer the holy eucharist with the utmost care and reverence?
R. I am.

4. All stand. The candidates kneel and the celebrant invites the faithful to pray:

Dear friends in Christ,
Let us pray with confidence to the Father; let us ask him to bestow his blessings on our brothers and sisters, chosen to be ministers of the eucharist.

Pause for silent prayer. the celebrant then continues:

Merciful Father,
creator and guide of your family,
bless ✠ our brothers and sisters N and N.
May they faithfully give the bread of life
to your people.
Strengthened by this sacrament,
may they come at last
to the banquet of heaven.
We ask this through Christ our Lord.
R. Amen.

5. The general intercessions should include an intention for the newly-commissioned ministers.

6. In the procession at the presentation of gifts the newly-commissioned ministers carry the vessels with the bread and wine, and at communion they receive the eucharist under both kinds.

B. Outside Mass

7. When the people are assembled an appropriate song is sung. The celebrant greets the people. There normally follows a short liturgy of the word. The readings and chants are taken, either in whole or in part, from the liturgy of the day.

8. The rite continues as above, nos. 2–5.

9. Finally, the celebrant blesses the people and dismisses them in the usual way. The rite concludes with an appropriate song.

Rite of Commissioning a Special Minister to Distribute Holy Communion on a Single Occasion

10. A person who, in a case of real necessity, is authorized to distribute the communion on a single occasion[2] should normally be commissioned according to the following rite.

11. During the breaking of the bread and the commingling, the person who is to distribute holy communion comes to the altar and stands before the celebrant. After the **Lamb of God** the priest blesses him/her with these words:

**Today you are to distribute
the body and blood of Christ
to your brothers and sisters.
May the Lord bless ✠ you, N.**
R. Amen.

12. When the priest has himself received communion in the usual way, he gives communion to the minister of the eucharist. Then he

gives him/her the paten or other vessel with the hosts. They then go to give communion to the people.

* This reference may be modified according to circumstances.
1 Instruction *Immensae caritatis* I, nos. 1, 6.
2 Instruction *Immensae caritatis* I, nos. 2, 6.

Excerpts from the English translation of the *Rite of Commissioning Special Ministers of Holy Communion* © 1978, International Committee on English in the Liturgy, Inc. All rights reserved.

Certificates for eucharistic ministers are available from Catholic book-shops or by post from the Carmelite Monastery, Quidenham, Norfolk (see Useful Addresses section at the back of the book). They serve to remind us of the serious undertaking we have made. Being dated, they also remind us that we must be recommissioned annually.

Recommissioning of lay eucharistic ministers

Because new ministers are trained when necessary or convenient, there may not be a strict calendar year between our commissioning and first recommissioning – the gap may be shorter. After that, we settle into a routine as communities tend to recommission ministers on the same Sunday or feast every year. If we miss the annual recom-missioning for some serious reason, we should make alternative arrangements as soon as possible, but may continue to minister in the interim.

For recommissioning, the above commissioning rite may be adapted as follows:

- omit the address to the lay ministers
- change the questions to: 'Are you resolved to continue to . . .'
- another question may be added, such as, 'Are you resolved to continue to deepen your understanding of the eucharistic mystery and express it more fully in the way you live?'
- change the prayer to: '. . . to continue to bestow his blessings . . .' and 'May they continue faithfully to give the bread of life . . .'

If the rite is not celebrated within Mass, it must be preceded by a short liturgy of the word.

Alternative rites of blessing for liturgical ministers (approved for interim use in England and Wales) will be found in the *Book of Blessings*. Copies of the texts are available from the Liturgy Office of the Bishops' Conference (the address is given in the Useful Addresses section at the back of the book).

At the Mass of the Lord's Supper on Maundy Thursday, a few parishes invite *all* their ministers, liturgical and other, to renew their commitment to serve, immediately after the washing of the feet. The priest addresses one question to each group in turn. A suitable text for the eucharistic ministers is as follows.

Eucharistic ministers, will you continue to give the body and blood of Christ to your brothers and sisters with love and respect?

R / We will.

A final thought . . .

> Ministers of the Eucharist are many;
> truly eucharistic ministers
> are what you must become.
> Let your service at the Lord's table
> make of your life
> a table of mercy and welcome
> for all you know and meet.

From Austin Fleming, *Yours is a Share:*
The call of liturgical ministry
(The Pastoral Press, 1985)

... and a prayer

Father, all-powerful and ever-living God,
we do well always and everywhere to give you thanks
through Jesus Christ our Lord.

At the last supper,
as he sat at table with his apostles,
he offered himself to you as the spotless lamb,
the acceptable gift that gives you perfect praise.
Christ has given us this memorial of his passion
to bring us its saving power until the end of time.

In this great sacrament you feed your people
and strengthen them in holiness,
so that the human family
may come to walk in the light of one faith,
in one communion of love.
We come then to this wonderful sacrament
to be fed at your table
and grow into the likeness of the risen Christ.

Earth unites with heaven
to sing the new song of creation
as we adore and praise you for ever.

Questions to ponder and discuss

If you are meeting as a group, continue with a planning session:

~best day and time for your day of recollection
~venue (and transport, if necessary)
~speaker
~theme of the day
~kind of group prayer
~outline timetable.

If you are reading this on your own, what would be your ideal day of recollection? Where, when, theme of the talks, guest speaker . . . ?

Further Information on Key Liturgical Points

Equal opportunities

Parishes may have to solve various difficulties to make liturgical ministry genuinely open to all.

Recent legislation requires better access for those with mobility difficulties. When handrails and ramps are being installed, we should consider the sanctuary area also. Loop sound systems should be standard in all churches. Good, considered lighting, without glare, helps both those with limited vision and those who lip-read. Such adaptations benefit all worshippers, not just the eucharistic ministers, and make for better liturgy.

Unspoken prejudices occasionally reveal themselves in our choice of eucharistic ministers. Ideally, ministers should reflect the parish mix of nationalities, age and appearance, educational achievements, class and wealth (or lack of it). However, we cannot pick people simply to fill gaps in a span of representative groups. Rather, our eucharistic ministers should be varied enough to make it clear that everyone is welcome, nobody is excluded on grounds of their colour or circumstances. In extreme cases, prejudice must be directly addressed. Somebody who will receive Communion from a white person but not a black one, for example, is dishonouring the sacrament.

Young adults may be invited to become eucharistic ministers once they have been confirmed (unless diocesan regulations set a minimum age limit). There is no official retirement age – we simply stop when we no longer feel comfortable ministering. Few people have perfect health, so if we manage to organize work and leisure around our medical needs, almost certainly we can include liturgical ministry, too.

Unless we can be flexible about the rota and organizing training sessions and meetings, we may exclude sections of the community from ministry. Those who work unsocial hours or variable shifts have much to offer, being available when those in other kinds of jobs are not. Equally, help with childcare can enable single parents to become liturgical ministers.

Above all, we must allow potential ministers to be themselves. Nothing is more prejudicial than making assumptions about others. Busy people may still want to take on something more, and have the time management skills to do it. On the other hand, the newly retired are not all looking for activities to fill their time.

The rules about receiving Communion

The act of receiving Communion is a reconciliation with God and the Church. We cannot approach the Lord's table, except as repentant sinners. Our daily failings damage our relationship with God a little, but do not destroy it, and frequent Communion is itself healing. Although it is a good habit to confess our sins every so often (once a year as a minimum) for the help and strength it gives us, we are only obliged to go to confession before Communion if we commit a very grave sin indeed.

Older people may remember fasting from midnight when they planned to receive Communion. It was a matter of respect and devotion to receive Communion before any other food that day. Later, when evening Masses were restored, the fast was reduced to three hours. Now we must deny ourselves food and drink (including sweets and gum!) for a mere one hour, and even then we may take water and medication at any time. The rule has been relaxed still further for the sick, who need wait only 15 minutes. Few people count the minutes exactly – we assume that by the time we've got to church and through Sunday Mass to the Communion rite, an hour has passed. This may be why we sometimes forget about the eucharistic fast altogether, which is a pity. If nothing else, being watchful that we eat or drink nothing is a useful transitional mechanism to prepare us for the Eucharist.

Most active lay people are content to take part in the liturgy and receive Communion once in a day. However, if we should happen to attend two distinct celebrations in one day (say Sunday Mass in the morning and a confirmation Mass in the afternoon), we may receive Communion at both.

As a general rule, non-Catholic Christians may not receive Communion in a Catholic church. To receive Communion is to claim to be 'in communion' and thus to accept the beliefs, teachings, rules and customs of the celebrating community. There are exceptions, for pastoral reasons, at the local bishop's discretion. In a similar way, Catholics should not receive Communion in a non-Catholic church.

Communion under both kinds

One of the changes to follow Vatican II was that lay people were once again offered the chalice as well as the consecrated bread. They were encouraged to receive Communion 'under both kinds', that is, in the form of bread *and* wine. This was not new, but it was something lay people had got out of the habit of doing for many centuries and had forgotten about. The practice was reintroduced slowly and only on special occasions at first, but parishes were soon offering Communion under both kinds at every Mass. Now it is so usual that we may feel deprived if we happen to visit a community where it is still not the custom.

Christ is fully present in the consecrated bread, so we cannot receive him more fully by receiving under both kinds. However, we can bring out the richness of the sacramental signs. The Eucharist is both sacrifice and meal. The bread that is broken signifies Christ's body, given for us on the cross; the wine signifies his blood shed for us. Bread is also our staple food, made from grain gathered from many plants and ground together. Drinking wine together signifies joyful celebration. In moderate quantities it is also thought to have healing qualities. Such signs help to draw us more deeply into the eucharistic mystery.

At the Last Supper, the apostles were invited both to 'Take and eat', and later, 'Take and drink.' Jesus did not think the bread alone was sufficient. He had told them, 'Anyone who does eat my flesh and drink my blood has eternal life' (John 6:54, NJB). Jesus has given himself for us with wide-armed generosity, and he wants us to receive him in the same way. Of course, nobody should feel coerced into receiving Communion under both kinds.

Indeed, there are a few occasions when Communion under one kind is advisable. A sick person may find it easier to receive a drop of the consecrated wine on the tongue, when swallowing solids is difficult. Wine does not keep for very long once exposed to air, so the precious blood is not usually reserved for future use. At services in the absence of a priest, therefore, Communion will be given in form of bread alone, using hosts consecrated some time previously.

Financial considerations, the extra time needed to give Communion under both kinds and the logistics of it are not good reasons to give Communion under only one kind.

Communion in the hand

We have seen that the first Christians touched and carried the eucharistic bread with both respect and confidence. We are fortunate to have the catecheses given by Cyril, bishop of Jerusalem in the fourth century, to the newly baptized. In one of them, he talks about the practicalities of receiving the host at Communion.

When the practice of receiving Communion in the hand was revived, Cyril's method was strongly recommended and has become standard. It is both safe and respectful; it is also far more ceremonious and meaningful than taking the consecrated bread directly with the fingers.

When you come forward, do not draw near with your hands wide open or with the fingers spread apart; instead, with your left hand make a throne for the right hand, which will receive the King. Receive the body of Christ in the hollow of your hand and give the response: 'Amen.'

Cyril, Catechesis 23, 22, as translated by Matthew J. O'Connell

Priests and presbyters

According to Peter, we are all, in Christ, a 'holy priesthood' (1 Peter 2:4, NJB) and the Book of Revelation also calls us a 'kingdom of priests' (1:6, NJB) . When it is necessary to avoid confusion with this common priesthood of all believers, the ordained priest is generally called a 'presbyter'. However, in ordinary parish life, 'priest' implies the ordained ministry and that is the usage adopted here.

Glossary of Terms Used in This Book

Altar cloth   A plain cloth of linen or cotton that covers the whole surface of the altar.

Altar linens   The collective term for all the cloths used in the Mass.

Altar vessels   The collective term for the various cups, dishes and so on used in the Mass.

Chalice   A stemmed 'cup', most often crafted of precious metals, which contains the wine that becomes the blood of the Lord. Some parishes also use a pouring chalice, which has a very large bowl with a lip. This offers the potent symbol of 'one cup' during the eucharistic prayer, but allows the contents to be transferred safely to several smaller chalices for Communion.

Ciborium   A lidded bowl, sometimes chalice-shaped, used to store consecrated hosts for later distribution.

Corporal   A smaller, square cloth placed on the altar cloth during the eucharistic liturgy. On it are placed the eucharistic gifts.

Credence table   A small serving table within the sanctuary area. Extra Communion dishes and chalices may be placed there before Mass, ready for Communion, and the empty vessels are returned there (not to the altar) after Communion.

Cruets   The wine and a small quantity of water needed for the Eucharist are often brought to the altar in small jugs, collectively called cruets. A separate jug of water (plus bowl and towel) is generally provided for the washing of hands.

Host An altar bread prepared from wheat flour and water, without additives. The refined, thin, wafer-like white host is hardly recognizable as bread, so thick, chewy, brown hosts are growing in popularity. To emphasize the 'one body' symbolism, large hosts, which can be broken into up to 50 portions, are preferable to individual small hosts.

Paten A flat or lipped plate on which the host is placed. With the introduction of large, thick altar breads, many parishes prefer to use deeper Communion dishes or bowls to prevent any pieces falling off.

Purificator A small napkin that is used to wipe the chalice and catch any drips. This is a functional item that will get stained and creased and should be laundered after every use.

Pyx A small, tight-lidded box used to carry the consecrated bread to the sick.

Tabernacle A strong steel safe – often beautifully decorated externally – in which the consecrated elements are reserved for Communion of the sick and for personal devotion.

Viaticum 'Food for the journey' to eternal life – the last Communion given to a person who is dying. It may be combined with sacramental reconciliation and the anointing of the sick if a priest is available.

Wine Altar wine must be made from pure grape juice, without additives, and have a specified alcohol content. It may be red or white. When only the priest received from the chalice, the wine was often fortified so it would keep. This is unnecessary when the whole community receives Communion under both kinds as this empties a bottle quickly.

Further Reading and Resources

Key documents

Vatican II, *Sacrosanctum Concilium* (*The Constitution on the Sacred Liturgy*), 1963

General Instruction on the Roman Missal (1970)
At the time of writing (July 2003), an English text for England and Wales of the third edition of the *General Instruction of the Roman Missal* is awaiting approval. Readers are urged to check this document, when published, for the latest directives.

Eucharisticum Mysterium (*Sacred Congregation of Rites*), 1967

Eucharistiae Sacramentum (*Sacred Congregation for Divine Worship*), 1973

Immensae Caritatis (*Sacred Congregation for the Discipline of the Sacraments*), 1973

English translations of the above documents can all be found in *Documents of Vatican II*, Austin P. Flannery (ed.), Eerdmans, 1975. They are also on the Vatican website (see the Useful Addresses section).

Canon Law Society of Great Britain and Ireland (tr.), *Code of Canon Law*, Collins, 1983
Canons 224 – 231 relate to the laity, canons 897 – 958 to the Eucharist.

Directory on Sunday Celebrations in the Absence of a Priest, Congregation for Divine Worship, 1988

One Bread, One Body, Bishops' Conference of England and Wales, 1998

On ministry in general

Bernadin, Cardinal Joseph, *The Ministry of Service*, The Liturgical Press, 1985
An introduction to ministry.

Fleming, Austin, *Yours is a Share*, The Pastoral Press, 1985

For eucharistic ministers

Kwatera OSB, Michael, *The Ministry of Communion*, The Liturgical Press, 1983

Study Book for Special Ministers of Holy Communion, Catholic Truth Society, 1980

Winstone, Harold, *Communion Under Both Kinds: Its significance*, Catholic Truth Society, 1979

Withey, Donald A., *Ministers of Holy Communion*, Decani, 1990
  A practical and liturgical guide.

Withey, Donald A., *Why Receive the Chalice?*, Kevin Mayhew, 1990

The Worship of the Eucharist, Catholic Truth Society (regularly reprinted)

Rites

Book of Blessings, The Liturgical Press, 1989

Celebrations of Word and Communion, Bishops' Conference of England and Wales, 1998

Communion of the Sick, McCrimmons (regularly reprinted)

Handbook for Special Ministers of Communion, Catholic Truth Society, 1982
  Contains commissioning rites for ministers, Communion of the sick and *viaticum*.

Order of Christian Funerals, 1995
Contains prayers for the dying, *viaticum* and so on.

Background reading

Cabié, Robert, *The Eucharist*, The Church at Prayer, Volume II, The Liturgical Press, 1986

The Catechism of the Catholic Church, Geoffrey Chapman, 1994
  Sections 1322 – 1419 deal with the Eucharist and earlier ones are on the liturgy in general.

Celebrating the Mass: a pastoral introduction, Bishops' Conference of England and Wales, 2003

Dean, Stephen (ed.), *Celebration: The liturgy handbook*, Geoffrey Chapman, 1993

Deiss CSSp, Lucien, *It's the Lord's Supper, the Eucharist of Christians*, Collins Liturgical, 1980

Mitchell OSB, Nathan, *Cult and Controversy: The worship of the Eucharist outside Mass*, Pueblo, 1982

Seasoltz, R. Kevin (ed.), *Living Bread, Saving Cup*, The Liturgical Press, 1982

Readings on the Eucharist

Stevenson, Kenneth W., *Eucharist and Offering*, Pueblo, 1986

For lay presiders

Cotter, Theresa, *Called To Preside*, St Anthony Messenger Press, 1997
  A handbook for lay people.

Hughes, Kathleen, *Lay Presiding: The art of leading prayer*, The Pastoral Press, 1988

Useful Addresses

Liturgy Office
Catholic Bishops' Conference of England and Wales
39 Eccleston Square
London SW1V 1PL
Tel: 020 7901 4850
Website: www.liturgy.demon.co.uk
e-mail: lifeworsh@cbcew.org.uk

Liturgical Commission/Council for my own diocese

Contact person:	
Address:	
Tel:	
e-mail:	

Vatican documents online
Website: www.vatican.va and follow the links

Other useful websites
Due to the nature of the medium, URLs change frequently. If you have trouble with any of these, search using the name of the parent organization.

Notre Dame Center for Pastoral Liturgy
Website: www.nd.edu/~ndcpl

Order of St Benedict
Website: www.osb.org/liturgy

Catholic Internet Directory
Website: www.catholic.net/RCC/Indices/index.html

Certificates for eucharistic ministers
Carmelite Monastery
Quidenham
Norwich
Norfolk NR16 2PH
Tel: 01953 887202
Website: www.carmelite.org.uk/Quidenham.html

Essential Information

The following table is intended as a useful place to record all the key contact details you need when you are a eucharistic minister.

Parish	*Tel:*
	e-mail:
Eucharistic ministers' leader	*Name:*
	Tel:
	e-mail:
Rota organizer (if different)	*Name:*
	Tel:
	e-mail:
Fellow ministers	*Name:*
	Tel:
	e-mail:
	Name:
	Tel:
	e-mail:
	Name:
	Tel:
	e-mail:
	Name:
	Tel:
	e-mail:
	Name:
	Tel:
	e-mail: